Top 20 Test Taking Tips

1. Carefully follow all the test registration procedures

2. Know the test directions, duration, topics, question types, how many questions

3. Setup a flexible study schedule at least 3-4 weeks before test day

4. Study during the time of day you are most alert, relaxed, and stress free

5. Maximize your learning style; visual learner use visual study aids, auditory learner use auditory study aids

6. Focus on your weakest knowledge base

7. Find a study partner to review with and help clarify questions

8. Practice, practice, practice

9. Get a good night's sleep; don't try to cram the night before the test

10. Eat a well balanced meal

11. Know the exact physical location of the testing site; drive the route to the site prior to test day

12. Bring a set of ear plugs; the testing center could be noisy

13. Wear comfortable, loose fitting, layered clothing to the testing center; prepare for it to be either cold or hot during the test

14. Bring at least 2 current forms of ID to the testing center

15. Arrive to the test early; be prepared to wait and be patient

16. Eliminate the obviously wrong answer choices, then guess the first remaining choice

17. Pace yourself; don't rush, but keep working and move on if you get stuck

18. Maintain a positive attitude even if the test is going poorly

19. Keep your first answer unless you are positive it is wrong

20. Check your work, don't make a careless mistake

The Listening Section

The Listening test of the TOEFL consists of a total of 30-50 questions.

There are three types of questions:
1. short conversations
2. long conversations and class discussions
3. lectures

You will have a headset that will allow you to adjust the volume of the recording. Short conversations will begin with a picture to provide orientation. With longer conversations and lectures, you will be provided with several pictures and visual cues.

Use the Pictures

The pictures are provided in order to orient you to the atmosphere and environment that the speakers and conducting their conversation. Use those pictures as much as possible. Try to put yourself in that environment. Become one of the pictured speakers and you will be able to better appreciate the conversation and what it means.

Use Multiple Inputs

The questions will be read to you at the same time they are exposed on the screen in the form of text. Take advantage of this. Use both the visual and auditory information being presented to better understand what is being asked. Some people are better visual and some better auditory receivers of information. Since both methods of presenting questions are given, use them both to your maximum advantage.

Main Ideas

Important words and main ideas in conversation are ones that will come up again and again. Listen carefully for any word or words that come up repeatedly. What words come up in nearly every statement made? These words with high frequency are likely to be in the main idea of the conversation. For example, in a conversation about class size in the business department of a college, the term "class size" is likely to appear in nearly every statement made by either speaker in the discussion.

Voice Changes

TOEFL expects you to be able to recognize and interpret nuances of speech. Be on the alert for any changes in voice, which might register surprise, excitement, or another emotion. If a speaker is talking in a normal monotone voice and suddenly raises their voice to a high pitch, that is a huge clue that something critical is being stated. Listen for a speaker to change their voice and understand the meaning of what they are saying.

Example:

Man: Let's go to Wal-mart.

Woman: *There's a Wal-mart in this small town?*

If the woman's statement was higher pitched, indicating surprise and shock, then she probably did not expect there to be a Wal-mart in that town.

Specifics

Listen carefully for specific pieces of information. Adjectives are commonly asked about in TOEFL questions. Try to remember any main adjectives that are mentioned. Pick out adjectives such as numbers, colors, or sizes.

Example:

Man: Let's go to the store and get some apples to make the pie.

Woman: How many do we need?

Man: We'll need **five** apples to make the pie.

A typical question might be about how many apples were needed.

Interpret

As you are listening to the conversation, put yourself in the person's shoes. Think about why someone would make a statement. You'll need to do more than just regurgitate the spoken words but also interpret them.

Example:

Woman: I think I'm sick with the flu.

Man: Why don't you go see the campus doctor?

Sample Question: Why did the man mention the campus doctor?

Answer: The campus doctor would be able to determine if the woman had the flu.

Find the Hidden Meaning

Look for the meaning behind a statement. When a speaker answers a question with a statement that doesn't immediately seem to answer the question, the response probably contained a hidden meaning that you will need to recognize and explain.

Man: Are you going to be ready for your presentation?

Woman: I've only got half of it finished and it's taken me five hours just to do this much. There's only an hour left before the presentation is due.

At first, the woman did not seem to answer the question the man presented. She responded with a statement that only seemed loosely related. Once you look deeper, then you can find the true meaning of what she said. If it took the woman five hours to do the first half of the presentation, then it would logically take her another five hours to do the second half. Since she only has one hour until her presentation is due, she would probably NOT be able to be ready for the presentation. So, while an answer was not immediately visible to the man's question, when you applied some logic to her response, you could find the hidden meaning beneath.

Longer Conversation Problem Types

Academic Conversations

Academic conversations are conversations on a college campus between professors, students, and other campus members. You will need to be able to summarize main ideas and recall important details.

Class Discussions

Class discussions are conversations in a classroom between professors and students. You will need to be able to summarize main ideas, but usually NOT need to recall important details.

Academic Talks

Academic Talks are conversations in an orientation meeting on academic courses and procedures or where a professor might discuss a variety of college topics. You will need to be able to summarize main ideas, but usually NOT need to recall important details.

Lectures

Lectures are conversations in a classroom about academic topics. You will need to be able to summarize main ideas, and be able to answer questions such as: who, what, when, where, or why?

The Speaking Section

You will be scored on how well you are able to communicate effectively in English.

Of all the test sections on the TOEFL, this is the easiest to prepare for. This is the test section that you can practice anywhere, in your car, in your room, on the phone, by yourself or with someone else. After you successfully pass TOEFL, you will be speaking English a lot, so you might as well prepare by speaking it at every opportunity beforehand.

Exhausting the Possibilities

You will be asked some basic questions. There are only so many possible basic questions that can be asked about someone. You can easily be prepared for every possibility. Go through and write down all the possibilities and a good answer for each. When you're asked about your family, don't have to struggle to come up with descriptions for your family members. Practice ahead of time and know what you're going to say. Right now as you're reading this, stop and take a minute to answer each of these following questions. If you were asked these in an interview, what would you say?

1. Please describe yourself.
2. Please describe your family.
3. Please describe your home.
4. Please describe some of your interests.
5. Please describe your job.
6. Please describe your studies

This is important practice. Make sure that you can spend a minute or so answering each of these questions without having to take time to think of a good response. These are basic questions and you should have your basic answers ready.

Tell a Story

Movie making is a multi-billion dollar industry. Why? It's because everyone likes to hear a good story, and the best movies contain great stories. The Speaking section interview can be a big aggravation for both sides. Usually, it is tense, uncomfortable, and boring for both the interviewer and the test taker.

Think about your favorite relatives. In many cases, they are your favorite because they are such raconteurs, or good storytellers. These are your aunts and uncles that can turn a simple trip to the grocery store into high adventure and will keep you captivated and entertained. Even if you're not a natural storyteller, with a little thought and practice, even you can turn your dull past experiences into exciting exploits.

Stories are your strongest weapon for captivating the interviewer and demonstrating your mastery of speaking English. Some questions literally beg for stories to be told. These need to be compelling stories, real time drama, and you're the hero. You want the interviewer begging for more, asking follow-up questions, eager to hear how it ends. Once you begin a quick exciting story, you set the tone of the interview, and you will determine what will be the follow-up questions.

The easiest way to prepare for these more difficult questions is to scour your memory for any exciting instance in your past. Perhaps where you played a leadership role or accomplished a goal. These can be from any part of your past, during your education, at home with your family, projects at work, or anything that you might have had a part in. Identify the main characteristics of the story, you want to have things straight. Make sure you know the basics of what happened, who was involved, why it occurred, and how the events unfolded sequentially. You certainly don't want to stumble over the facts and repeat yourself during the interview.

One Size Fits All

These basic stories are building blocks. Just as a piece of lumber can be cut into many different shapes and have many completely unique uses, each of your stories does not only answer one unique question. Your stories are one size fits all. With practice you will find that you can use the same story to answer two seemingly unrelated questions.

For example, a question about teamwork and working under pressure can both be answered by a story about your experience playing intramural basketball. The story could describe how you had to work as a team in order to get into the playoffs, spending time practicing together, coordinating plays, whatever was necessary for the team to advance. Alternatively, the story could focus upon the clutch shots that you made that season in order to win the game in the last few seconds of play under enormous pressure. The basic story is the same: your experiences playing basketball.

The questions were different, but you customized the story to fit the question. With practice you should be able to answer almost any question with just a few stock stories that can be customized.

Find the Bridges

Some questions will lend themselves more readily to a story than others. You must have a set of basic stories ready that can be modified to fit the occasion. You must "find the bridges" in the questions offered to make sure your stories get told.

In WWII, the US Army used Bailey bridges. Bailey bridges were bridges made of prefabricated steel sections that were carried around and could be thrown together at a moment's notice, allowing the army to move quickly across any obstacle and get to where they wanted to go.

You need to find bridges, i.e. opportunities to tell your stories. Look for any chance to turn a standard question about anything, into a bridge to begin telling your story. For example, "What is your job title?"

On the surface that might not seem like the ideal bridge, but with a little insight your response might become:

"My job title is Product Line Manager. I was responsible for everything from the development of new products, to the obsolescence of old products. Marketing, sales, engineering, and production of the entire product line fell under my responsibility. One of the products was even my own idea based on feedback I received from my interactions with our customers. In the first year, it alone had achieved a sales level of over…"

The key to remember is that just because a question is asked as a closed ended question (yes/no, or one word answers), doesn't mean that you have to answer it as a closed ended question. Answer the question asked, but then find a way to develop your answer and a bridge to a good story of yours. With an open mind, the most closed ended of questions can become a launch pad into a story.

Pregnant Pause

A good story can usually wind its way down a long path. There is always a danger that you will begin to bore the interviewer, who may wonder if an end is in sight. Some interviewers may get worried that they won't be able to get through the fifteen questions on their list during the allotted time. Therefore, find natural breaks in your story and pause for a second. If the interviewer maintains eye contact or asks continuation questions, then keep going. But this will give them a chance to stop the story and ask a different question if they are getting bored and want to move on.

Practice Makes Perfect

Don't try to answer every question by shooting from the hip. You'll spend most of your time trying to think of what happened and repeating yourself. Think of the classic stories that you could tell and then practice going over them with your friends, explaining how you successfully achieved the goal, or took charge and gave leadership to your group project. You don't want to have the story memorized, because it will become stale in the telling, but you want it to be smooth. This story must be live and in living color, where the interviewer can see himself taking part on the sidelines and watching the situation take place. Have your friends and family members quiz you by asking you random questions and see how well you can adapt to the question and give a lucid response.

The Reading Section

The Reading section of the TOEFL consists of a total of 44-60 questions.

There are three to six passages, which will each be followed by an average of six to ten questions.

Reading Comprehension

Understanding Literature

Reading literature is a different experience than reading non-fiction works. Our imagination is more active as we review what we have read, imagine ourselves as characters in the novel, and try to guess what will happen next. Suspense, surprise, fantasy, fear, anxiety, compassion, and a host of other emotions and feelings may be stirred by a provocative novel.

Reading longer works of fiction is a cumulative process. Some elements of a novel have a great impact, while others may go virtually unnoticed. Therefore, as novels are read with a critical eye to language, it is helpful to perceive and identify larger patterns and movements in the work as a whole. This will benefit the reader by placing characters and events in perspective, and will enrich the reading experience greatly. Novels should be savored rather than gulped. Careful reading and thoughtful analysis of the major themes of the novel are essential to a clear understanding of the work.

One of the most important skills in reading comprehension is the identification of **topics** and **main ideas.** There is a subtle difference between these two features. The topic is the subject of a text, or what the text is about. The main idea, on the other hand, is the most important point being made by the author. The topic is usually expressed in a few words at the most, while the main idea often needs a full sentence to be completely defined. As an example, a short passage might have the topic of penguins and the main idea *Penguins are different from other birds in many ways.* In most nonfiction writing, the topic

- 15 -

and the main idea will be stated directly, often in a sentence at the very beginning or end of the text. When being tested on an understanding of the author's topic, the reader can quickly *skim* the passage for the general idea, stopping to read only the first sentence of each paragraph. A paragraph's first sentence is often (but not always) the main topic sentence, and it gives you a summary of the content of the paragraph. However, there are cases in which the reader must figure out an unstated topic or main idea. In these instances, the student must read every sentence of the text, and try to come up with an overarching idea that is supported by each of those sentences.

While the main idea is the overall premise of a story, **supporting details** provide evidence and backing for the main point. In order to show that a main idea is correct, or valid, the author needs to add details that prove their point. All texts contain details, but they are only classified as supporting details when they serve to reinforce some larger point. Supporting details are most commonly found in informative and persuasive texts. In some cases, they will be clearly indicated with words like *for example* or *for instance*, or they will be enumerated with words like *first*, *second*, and *last*. However, they may not be indicated with special words. As a reader, it is important to consider whether the author's supporting details really back up his or her main point. Supporting details can be factual and correct but still not relevant to the author's point. Conversely, supporting details can seem pertinent but be ineffective because they are based on opinion or assertions that cannot be proven.

An example of a main idea is: "Giraffes live in the Serengeti of Africa." A supporting detail about giraffes could be: "A giraffe uses its long neck to reach twigs and leaves on trees." The main idea gives the general idea that the text is about giraffes. The supporting detail gives a specific fact about how the giraffes eat.

As opposed to a main idea, themes are seldom expressed directly in a text, so they can be difficult to identify. A **theme** is an issue, an idea, or a question raised by the text. For instance, a theme of William Shakespeare's *Hamlet* is indecision, as the title character explores his own psyche and the results of his failure to make bold choices. A great work of literature may have many themes, and the reader is justified in identifying any for which he or she can find support. One common characteristic of themes is that they raise more questions than they answer. In a good piece of fiction, the author is not always trying to convince the reader, but is instead trying to elevate the reader's perspective and encourage him to consider the themes more deeply. When reading, one can identify themes by constantly asking what general issues the text is addressing. A good way to evaluate an author's approach to a theme is to begin reading with a question in mind (for example, how does this text approach the theme of love?) and then look for evidence in the text that addresses that question.

Purposes for Writing

In order to be an effective reader, one must pay attention to the author's **position** and purpose. Even those texts that seem objective and impartial, like textbooks, have some sort of position and bias. Readers need to take these positions into account when considering the author's message. When an author uses emotional language or clearly favors one side of an argument, his position is clear. However, the author's position may be evident not only in what he writes, but in what he doesn't write. For this reason, it is sometimes necessary to review some other texts on the same topic in order to develop a view of the author's position. If this is not possible, then it may be useful to acquire a little background personal information about the author. When the only source of information is the text, however, the reader should look for language and argumentation that seems to indicate a particular stance on the subject.

Identifying the **purpose** of an author is usually easier than identifying her position. In most cases, the author has no interest in hiding his or her purpose. A text that is meant to entertain, for instance, should be obviously written to please the reader. Most narratives, or stories, are written to entertain, though they may also inform or persuade. Informative texts are easy to identify as well. The most difficult purpose of a text to identify is persuasion, because the author has an interest in making this purpose hard to detect. When a person knows that the author is trying to convince him, he is automatically more wary and skeptical of the argument. For this reason persuasive texts often try to establish an entertaining tone, hoping to amuse the reader into agreement, or an informative tone, hoping to create an appearance of authority and objectivity.

An author's purpose is often evident in the organization of the text. For instance, if the text has headings and subheadings, if key terms are in bold, and if the author makes his main idea clear from the beginning, then the likely purpose of the text is to inform. If the author begins by making a claim and then makes various arguments to support that claim, the purpose is probably to persuade. If the author is telling a story, or is more interested in holding the attention of the reader than in making a particular point or delivering information, then his purpose is most likely to entertain. As a reader, it is best to judge an author on how well he accomplishes his purpose. In other words, it is not entirely fair to complain that a textbook is boring: if the text is clear and easy to understand, then the author has done his job. Similarly, a storyteller should not be judged too harshly for getting some facts wrong, so long as he is able to give pleasure to the reader.

The author's purpose for writing will affect his writing style and the response of the reader. In a **persuasive essay**, the author is attempting to change the reader's mind or convince him of something he did not believe previously. There are several identifying characteristics of persuasive writing. One is opinion presented as fact. When an author attempts to persuade the reader, he often presents his or her opinions as if they were fact. A reader must be on guard for statements that sound factual but which cannot be subjected to research, observation, or experiment. Another characteristic of persuasive writing is emotional language. An author will often try to play on the reader's emotion by appealing to his sympathy or sense of morality. When an author uses colorful or evocative language with the intent of arousing the reader's passions, it is likely that he is attempting to persuade. Finally, in many cases a persuasive text will give an unfair explanation of opposing positions, if these positions are mentioned at all.

An **informative text** is written to educate and enlighten the reader. Informative texts are almost always nonfiction, and are rarely structured as a story. The intention of an informative text is to deliver information in the most comprehensible way possible, so the structure of the text is likely to be very clear. In an informative text, the thesis statement is often in the first sentence. The author may use some colorful language, but is likely to put more emphasis on clarity and precision. Informative essays do not typically appeal to the emotions. They often contain facts and figures, and rarely include the opinion of the author. Sometimes a persuasive essay can resemble an informative essay, especially if the author maintains an even tone and presents his or her views as if they were established fact.

The success or failure of an author's intent to **entertain** is determined by those who read the author's work. Entertaining texts may be either fiction or nonfiction, and they may describe real or imagined people, places, and events. Entertaining texts are often narratives, or stories. A text that is written to entertain is likely to contain colorful language that engages the imagination and the emotions. Such writing often features a great deal of figurative language, which typically enlivens its subject matter with images and analogies. Though an entertaining text is not usually written to persuade or inform, it may accomplish both of these tasks. An entertaining text may appeal to the reader's emotions and cause him or her to think differently about a particular subject. In any case, entertaining texts tend to showcase the personality of the author more so than do other types of writing.

When an author intends to **express feelings,** she may use colorful and evocative language. An author may write emotionally for any number of reasons. Sometimes, the author will do so because she is describing a personal situation of great pain or happiness. Sometimes an author is attempting to persuade the reader, and so will use emotion to stir up the passions. It can be easy to identify this kind of expression when the writer uses phrases like *I felt* and *I sense*. However, sometimes the author will simply describe feelings without introducing them. As a reader, it is important to recognize when an author is expressing emotion, and not to become overwhelmed by sympathy or passion. A reader should maintain some detachment so that he or she can still evaluate the strength of the author's argument or the quality of the writing.

In a sense, almost all writing is descriptive, insofar as it seeks to describe events, ideas, or people to the reader. Some texts, however, are primarily concerned with **description**. A descriptive text focuses on a particular subject, and attempts to depict it in a way that will be clear to the reader. Descriptive texts contain many adjectives and adverbs, words that give shades of meaning and create a more detailed mental picture for the reader. A descriptive text fails when it is unclear or vague to the reader. On the other hand, however, a descriptive text that compiles too much detail can be boring and overwhelming to the reader. A descriptive text will certainly be informative, and it may be persuasive and entertaining as well. Descriptive writing is a challenge for the author, but when it is done well, it can be fun to read.

Writing Devices

Authors will use different stylistic and writing devices to make their meaning more clearly understood. One of those devices is comparison and contrast. When an author describes the ways in which two things are alike, he or she is **comparing** them. When the author describes the ways in which two things are different, he or she is **contrasting** them. The "compare and contrast" essay is one of the most common forms in nonfiction. It is often signaled with certain words: a comparison may be indicated with such words as *both*, *same*, *like*, *too*, and *as well*; while a contrast may be indicated by words like *but, however, on the other hand*, *instead*, and *yet*. Of course, comparisons and contrasts may be implicit without using any such signaling language. A single sentence may both compare and contrast. Consider the sentence *Brian and Sheila love ice cream, but Brian prefers vanilla and Sheila prefers strawberry*. In one sentence, the author has described both a similarity (love of ice cream) and a difference (favorite flavor).

One of the most common text structures is **cause and effect**. A cause is an act or event that makes something happen, and an effect is the thing that happens as a result of that cause. A cause-and-effect relationship is not always explicit, but there are some words in English that signal causality, such as *since*, *because*, and *as a result*. As an example, consider the sentence *Because the sky was clear, Ron did not bring an umbrella*. The cause is the clear sky, and the effect is that Ron did not bring an umbrella. However, sometimes the cause-and-effect relationship will not be clearly noted. For instance, the sentence *He was late and missed the meeting* does not contain any signaling words, but it still contains a cause (he was late) and an effect (he missed the meeting). It is possible for a single cause to have multiple effects, or for a single effect to have multiple causes. Also, an effect can in turn be the cause of another effect, in what is known as a cause-and-effect chain.

Authors often use analogies to add meaning to the text. An **analogy** is a comparison of two things. The words in the analogy are connected by a certain, often undetermined relationship. Look at this analogy: moo is to cow as quack is to duck. This analogy compares the sound that a cow makes with the sound that a duck makes. Even if the word 'quack' was not given, one could figure out it is the correct word to complete the analogy based on the relationship between the words 'moo' and 'cow'. Some common relationships for analogies include synonyms, antonyms, part to whole, definition, and actor to action.

Another element that impacts a text is the author's point of view. The **point of view** of a text is the perspective from which it is told. The author will always have a point of view about a story before he draws up a plot line. The author will know what events they want to take place, how they want the characters to interact, and how the story will resolve. An author will also have an opinion on the topic, or series of events, which is presented in the story, based on their own prior experience and beliefs.

The two main points of view that authors use are first person and third person. If the narrator of the story is also the main character, or *protagonist*, the text is written in first-person point of view. In first person, the author writes with the word *I*. Third-person point of view is probably the most common point of view that authors use. Using third person, authors refer to each character using the words *he* or *she.* In third-person omniscient, the narrator is not a character in the story and tells the story of all of the characters at the same time.

A good writer will use **transitional words** and phrases to guide the reader through the text. You are no doubt familiar with the common transitions, though you may never have considered how they operate. Some transitional phrases (*after, before, during, in the middle of*) give information about time. Some indicate that an example is about to be given (*for example, in fact, for instance*). Writers use them to compare (*also, likewise*) and contrast (*however, but, yet*). Transitional words and phrases can suggest addition (*and, also, furthermore, moreover*) and logical relationships (*if, then, therefore, as a result, since*). Finally, transitional words and phrases can demarcate the steps in a process (*first, second, last*). You should incorporate transitional words and phrases where they will orient your reader and illuminate the structure of your composition.

A **narrative** passage is a story. Narratives can be fiction or nonfiction. However, there are a few elements that a text must have in order to be classified as a narrative. To begin with, the text must have a plot. That is, it must describe a series of events. If it is a good narrative, these events will be interesting and emotionally engaging to the reader. A narrative also has characters. These could be people, animals, or even inanimate objects, so long as they participate in the plot. A narrative passage often contains figurative language, which is meant to stimulate the imagination of the reader by making comparisons and observations. A metaphor, which is a description of one thing in terms of another, is a common piece of figurative language. *The moon was a frosty snowball* is an example of a metaphor: it is obviously untrue in the literal sense, but it suggests a certain mood for the reader. Narratives often proceed in a clear sequence, but they do not need to do so.

An **expository** passage aims to inform and enlighten the reader. It is nonfiction and usually centers around a simple, easily defined topic. Since the goal of exposition is to teach, such a passage should be as clear as possible. It is common for an expository passage to contain helpful organizing words, like *first*, *next*, *for example*, and *therefore*. These words keep the reader oriented in the text. Although expository passages do not need to feature colorful language and artful writing, they are often more effective when they do. For a reader, the challenge of expository passages is to maintain steady attention. Expository passages are not always about subjects in which a reader will naturally be interested, and the writer is often more concerned with clarity and comprehensibility than with engaging the reader. For this reason, many expository passages are dull. Making notes is a good way to maintain focus when reading an expository passage.

A **technical** passage is written to describe a complex object or process. Technical writing is common in medical and technological fields, in which complicated mathematical, scientific, and engineering ideas need to be explained simply and clearly. To ease comprehension, a technical passage usually proceeds in a very logical order. Technical passages often have clear headings and subheadings, which are used to keep the reader oriented in the text. It is also common for these passages to break sections up with numbers or letters. Many technical passages look more like an outline than a piece of prose. The amount of jargon or difficult vocabulary will vary in a technical passage depending on the intended audience. As much as possible, technical passages try to avoid language that the reader will have to research in order to understand the message. Of course, it is not always possible to avoid jargon.

A **persuasive** passage is meant to change the reader's mind or lead her into agreement with the author. The persuasive intent may be obvious, or it may be quite difficult to discern. In some cases, a persuasive passage will be indistinguishable from an informative passage: it will make an assertion and offer supporting details. However, a persuasive passage is more likely to make claims based on opinion and to appeal to the reader's emotions. Persuasive passages may not describe alternate positions and, when they do, they often display significant bias. It may be clear that a persuasive passage is giving the author's viewpoint, or the passage may adopt a seemingly objective tone. A persuasive passage is successful if it can make a convincing argument and win the trust of the reader.

A persuasive essay will likely focus on one central argument, but it may make many smaller claims along the way. These are subordinate arguments with which the reader must agree if he or she is going to agree with the central argument. The central argument will only be as strong as the subordinate claims. These claims should be rooted in fact and observation, rather than subjective judgment. The best persuasive essays provide enough supporting detail to justify claims without overwhelming the reader. Remember that a fact must be susceptible to independent verification: that is, it must be something the reader could confirm. Also, statistics are only effective when they take into account possible objections. For instance, a statistic on the number of foreclosed houses would only be useful if it was taken over a defined interval and in a defined area. Most readers are wary of statistics, because they are so often misleading. If possible, a persuasive essay should always include references so that the reader can obtain more information. Of course, this means that the writer's accuracy and fairness may be judged by the inquiring reader.

Opinions are formed by emotion as well as reason, and persuasive writers often appeal to the feelings of the reader. Although readers should always be skeptical of this technique, it is often used in a proper and ethical manner. For instance, there are many subjects that have an obvious emotional component, and therefore cannot be completely treated without an appeal to the emotions. Consider an article on drunk driving: it makes sense to include some specific examples that will alarm or sadden the reader. After all, drunk driving often has serious and tragic consequences. Emotional appeals are not appropriate, however, when they attempt to mislead the reader. For instance, in political advertisements it is common to emphasize the patriotism of the preferred candidate, because this will encourage the audience to link their own positive feelings about the country with their opinion of the candidate. However, these ads often imply that the other candidate is unpatriotic, which in most cases is far from the truth. Another common and improper emotional appeal is the use of loaded language, as for instance referring to an avidly religious person as a "fanatic" or a passionate environmentalist as a "tree hugger." These terms introduce an emotional component that detracts from the argument.

History and Culture

Historical context has a profound influence on literature: the events, knowledge base, and assumptions of an author's time color every aspect of his or her work. Sometimes, authors hold opinions and use language that would be considered inappropriate or immoral in a modern setting, but that was acceptable in the author's time. As a reader, one should consider how the historical context influenced a work and also how today's opinions and ideas shape the way modern readers read the works of the past. For instance, in most societies of the past, women were treated as second-class citizens. An author who wrote in 18th-century England might sound sexist to modern readers, even if that author was relatively feminist in his time. Readers should not have to excuse the faulty assumptions and prejudices of the past, but they should appreciate that a person's thoughts and words are, in part, a result of the time and culture in which they live or lived, and it is perhaps unfair to expect writers to avoid all of the errors of their times.

Even a brief study of world literature suggests that writers from vastly different cultures address similar themes. For instance, works like the *Odyssey* and *Hamlet* both tackle the individual's battle for self-control and independence. In every culture, authors address themes of personal growth and the struggle for maturity. Another universal theme is the conflict between the individual and society. In works as culturally disparate as *Native Son*, the *Aeneid*, and *1984*, authors dramatize how people struggle to maintain their personalities and dignity in large, sometimes oppressive groups. Finally, many cultures have versions of the hero's (or heroine's) journey, in which an adventurous person must overcome many obstacles in order to gain greater knowledge, power, and perspective. Some famous works that treat this theme are the *Epic of Gilgamesh*, Dante's *Divine Comedy*, and *Don Quixote*.

Authors from different genres (for instance poetry, drama, novel, short story) and cultures may address similar themes, but they often do so quite differently. For instance, poets are likely to address subject matter obliquely, through the use of images and allusions. In a play, on the other hand, the author is more likely to dramatize themes by using characters to express opposing viewpoints. This disparity is known as a dialectical approach. In a novel, the author does not need to express themes directly; rather, they can be illustrated through events and actions. In some regional literatures, like those of Greece or England, authors use more irony: their works have characters that express views and make decisions that are clearly disapproved of by the author. In Latin America, there is a great tradition of using supernatural events to illustrate themes about real life. In China and Japan, authors frequently use well-established regional forms (haiku, for instance) to organize their treatment of universal themes.

Responding to Literature

When reading good literature, the reader is moved to engage actively in the text. One part of being an active reader involves making predictions. A **prediction** is a guess about what will happen next. Readers are constantly making predictions based on what they have read and what they already know. Consider the following sentence: *Staring at the* *computer screen in shock, Kim blindly reached over for the brimming glass of water on the shelf to her side.* The sentence suggests that Kim is agitated and that she is not looking at the glass she is going to pick up, so a reader might predict that she is going to knock the glass over. Of course, not every prediction will be accurate: perhaps Kim will pick the glass up cleanly. Nevertheless, the author has certainly created the expectation that the water might be spilled. Predictions are always subject to revision as the reader acquires more information.

Test-taking tip: To respond to questions requiring future predictions, the student's answers should be based on evidence of past or present behavior.

Readers are often required to understand text that claims and suggests ideas without stating them directly. An **inference** is a piece of information that is implied but not written outright by the author. For instance, consider the following sentence: *Mark made more money that week than he had in the previous year.* From this sentence, the reader can infer that Mark either has not made much money in the previous year or made a great deal of money that week. Often, a reader can use information he or she already knows to make inferences. Take as an example the sentence *When his coffee arrived, he looked around the table for the silver cup.* Many people know that cream is typically served in a silver cup, so using their own base of knowledge they can infer that the subject of this sentence takes his coffee with cream. Making inferences requires concentration, attention, and practice.

Test-taking tip: While being tested on his ability to make correct inferences, the student must look for contextual clues. An answer can be *right* but not *correct*. The contextual clues will help you find the answer that is the best answer out of the given choices. Understand the context in which a phrase is stated. When asked for the implied meaning of a statement made in the passage, the student should immediately locate the statement and read the context in which it was made. Also, look for an answer choice that has a similar phrase to the statement in question.

A reader must be able to identify a text's **sequence**, or the order in which things happen. Often, and especially when the sequence is very important to the author, it is indicated with signal words like *first*, *then*, *next*, and *last*. However, sometimes a sequence is merely implied and must be noted by the reader. Consider the sentence *He walked in the* *front door and switched on the hall lamp*. Clearly, the man did not turn the lamp on before he walked in the door, so the implied sequence is that he first walked in the door and then turned on the lamp. Texts do not always proceed in an orderly sequence from first to last: sometimes, they begin at the end and then start over at the beginning. As a reader, it can be useful to make brief notes to clarify the sequence.

In addition to inferring and predicting things about the text, the reader must often **draw conclusions** about the information he has read. When asked for a *conclusion* that may be drawn, look for critical "hedge" phrases, such as *likely, may, can, will often,* among many others. When you are being tested on this knowledge, remember that question writers insert these hedge phrases to cover every possibility. Often an answer will be wrong simply because it leaves no room for exception. Extreme positive or negative answers (such as always, never, etc.) are usually not correct. The reader should not use any outside knowledge that is not gathered from the reading passage to answer the related questions. Correct answers can be derived straight from the reading passage.

Literary Genres

Literary genres refer to the basic generic types of poetry, drama, fiction, and nonfiction. Literary genre is a method of classifying and analyzing literature. There are numerous subdivisions within genre, including such categories as novels, novellas, and short stories in fiction. Drama may also be subdivided into comedy, tragedy, and many other categories. Poetry and nonfiction have their own distinct divisions.

Genres often overlap, and the distinctions among them are blurred, such as that between the nonfiction novel and docudrama, as well as many others. However, the use of genres is helpful to the reader as a set of understandings that guide our responses to a work. The generic norm sets expectations and forms the framework within which we read and evaluate a work. This framework will guide both our understanding and interpretation of the work. It is a useful tool for both literary criticism and analysis.

Fiction is a general term for any form of literary narrative that is invented or imagined rather than being factual. For those individuals who equate fact with truth, the imagined or invented character of fiction tends to render it relatively unimportant or trivial among the genres. Defenders of fiction are quick to point out that the fictional mode is an essential part of being. The ability to imagine or discuss what-if plots, characters, and events is clearly part of the human experience.

Prose is derived from the Latin and means "straightforward discourse." Prose fiction, although having many categories, may be divided into three main groups:

- **Short stories**: a fictional narrative, the length of which varies, usually under 20,000 words. Short stories usually have only a few characters and generally describe one major event or insight. The short story began in magazines in the late 1800s and has flourished ever since.

- **Novels**: a longer work of fiction, often containing a large cast of characters and extensive plotting. The emphasis may be on an event, action, social problems, or any experience. There is now a genre of nonfiction novels pioneered by Truman Capote's *In Cold Blood* in the 1960s. Novels may also be written in verse.

- **Novellas**: a work of narrative fiction longer than a short story but shorter than a novel. Novellas may also be called short novels or novelettes. They originated from the German tradition and have become common forms in all of the world's literature.

Many elements influence a work of prose fiction. Some important ones are:

- Speech and dialogue: Characters may speak for themselves or through the narrator. Dialogue may be realistic or fantastic, depending on the author's aim.

- Thoughts and mental processes: There may be internal dialogue used as a device for plot development or character understanding.

- Dramatic involvement: Some narrators encourage readers to become involved in the events of the story, whereas others attempt to distance readers through literary devices.

- Action: This is any information that advances the plot or involves new interactions between the characters.

- Duration: The time frame of the work may be long or short, and the relationship between described time and narrative time may vary.
- Setting and description: Is the setting critical to the plot or characters? How are the action scenes described?
- Themes: This is any point of view or topic given sustained attention.
- Symbolism: Authors often veil meanings through imagery and other literary constructions.

Fiction is much wider than simply prose fiction. Songs, ballads, epics, and narrative poems are examples of non-prose fiction. A full definition of fiction must include not only the work itself but also the framework in which it is read. Literary fiction can also be defined as not true rather than nonexistent, as many works of historical fiction refer to real people, places, and events that are treated imaginatively as if they were true. These imaginary elements enrich and broaden literary expression.

When analyzing fiction, it is important for the reader to look carefully at the work being studied. The plot or action of a narrative can become so entertaining that the language of the work is ignored. The language of fiction should not simply be a way to relate a plot—it should also yield many insights to the judicious reader. Some prose fiction is based on the reader's engagement with the language rather than the story. A studious reader will analyze the mode of expression as well as the narrative. Part of the reward of reading in this manner is to discover how the author uses different language to describe familiar objects, events, or emotions. Some works focus the reader on an author's unorthodox use of language, whereas others may emphasize characters or storylines. What happens in a story is not always the critical element in the work. This type of reading may be difficult at first but yields great rewards.

The **narrator** is a central part of any work of fiction, and can give insight about the purpose of the work and its main themes and ideas. The following are important questions to address to better understand the voice and role of the narrator and incorporate that voice into an overall understanding of the novel:

- Who is the narrator of the novel? What is the narrator's perspective, first person or third person? What is the role of the narrator in the plot? Are there changes in narrators or the perspective of narrators?

- Does the narrator explain things in the novel, or does meaning emerge from the plot and events? The personality of the narrator is important. She may have a vested interest in a character or event described. Some narratives follow the time sequence of the plot, whereas others do not. A narrator may express approval or disapproval about a character or events in the work.

- Tone is an important aspect of the narration. Who is actually being addressed by the narrator? Is the tone familiar or formal, intimate or impersonal? Does the vocabulary suggest clues about the narrator?

A **character** is a person intimately involved with the plot and development of the novel. Development of the novel's characters not only moves the story along but will also tell the reader a lot about the novel itself. There is usually a physical description of the character, but this is often omitted in modern and postmodern novels. These works may focus on the psychological state or motivation of the character. The choice of a character's name may give valuable clues to his role in the work.

Characters are said to be flat or round. Flat characters tend to be minor figures in the story, changing little or not at all. Round characters (those understood from a well-rounded view) are more central to the story and tend to change as the plot unfolds. Stock characters are similar to flat characters, filling out the story without influencing it.

Modern literature has been greatly affected by Freudian psychology, giving rise to such devices as the interior monologue and magical realism as methods of understanding characters in a work. These give the reader a more complex understanding of the inner lives of the characters and enrich the understanding of relationships between characters.

Another important genre is that of **drama**: a play written to be spoken aloud. The drama is in many ways inseparable from performance. Reading drama ideally involves using imagination to visualize and re-create the play with characters and settings. The reader stages the play in his imagination, watching characters interact and developments unfold. Sometimes this involves simulating a theatrical presentation; other times it involves imagining the events. In either case, the reader is imagining the unwritten to re-create the dramatic experience. Novels present some of the same problems, but a narrator will provide much more information about the setting, characters, inner dialogues, and many other supporting details. In drama, much of this is missing, and we are required to use our powers of projection and imagination to taste the full flavor of the dramatic work. There are many empty spaces in dramatic texts that must be filled by the reader to fully appreciate the work.

When reading drama in this way, there are some advantages over watching the play performed (though there is much criticism in this regard):

- Freedom of point of view and perspective: Text is free of interpretations of actors, directors, producers, and technical staging.
- Additional information: The text of a drama may be accompanied by notes or prefaces placing the work in a social or historical context. Stage directions may also provide relevant information about the author's purpose. None of this is typically available at live or filmed performances.
- Study and understanding: Difficult or obscure passages may be studied at leisure and supplemented by explanatory works. This is particularly true of older plays with unfamiliar language, which cannot be fully understood without an opportunity to study the material.

Critical elements of drama, especially when it is being read aloud or performed, include dialect, speech, and dialogue. Analysis of speech and dialogue is important in the critical study of drama. Some playwrights use speech to develop their characters. Speeches may be long or short, and written in as normal prose or blank verse. Some characters have a unique way of speaking which illuminates aspects of the drama. Emphasis and tone are both important, as well. Does the author make clear the tone in which lines are to be spoken, or is this open to interpretation? Sometimes there are various possibilities in tone with regard to delivering lines.

Dialect is any distinct variety of a language, especially one spoken in a region or part of a country. The criterion for distinguishing dialects from languages is that of mutual understanding. For example, people who speak Dutch cannot understand English unless they have learned it. But a speaker from Amsterdam can understand one from Antwerp; therefore, they speak different dialects of the same language. This is, however, a matter of degree; there are languages in which different dialects are unintelligible.

Dialect mixtures are the presence in one form of speech with elements from different neighboring dialects. The study of speech differences from one geographical area to another is called dialect geography. A dialect atlas is a map showing distribution of dialects in a given area. A dialect continuum shows a progressive shift in dialects across a territory, such that adjacent dialects are understandable, but those at the extremes are not.

Dramatic dialogue can be difficult to interpret and changes depending upon the tone used and which words are emphasized. Where the stresses, or meters, of dramatic dialogue fall can determine meaning. Variations in emphasis are only one factor in the manipulability of dramatic speech. Tone is of equal or greater importance and expresses a range of possible emotions and feelings that cannot be readily discerned from the script of a play. The reader must add tone to the words to understand the full meaning of a passage. Recognizing tone is a cumulative process as the reader begins to understand the characters and situations in the play. Other elements that influence the interpretation of dialogue include the setting, possible reactions of the characters to the speech, and possible gestures or facial expressions of the actor. There are no firm rules to guide the interpretation of dramatic speech. An open and flexible attitude is essential in interpreting dramatic dialogue.

Action is a crucial element in the production of a dramatic work. Many dramas contain little dialogue and much action. In these cases, it is essential for the reader to carefully study stage directions and visualize the action on the stage. Benefits of understanding stage directions include knowing which characters are on the stage at all times, who is speaking to whom, and following these patterns through changes of scene.

Stage directions also provide additional information, some of which is not available to a live audience. The nature of the physical space where the action occurs is vital, and stage directions help with this. The historical context of the period is important in understanding what the playwright was working with in terms of theaters and physical space. The type of staging possible for the author is a good guide to the spatial elements of a production.

Asides and soliloquies are devices that authors use in plot and character development. **Asides** indicate that not all characters are privy to the lines. This may be a method of advancing or explaining the plot in a subtle manner. **Soliloquies** are opportunities for character development, plot enhancement, and to give insight to characters motives, feelings, and emotions. Careful study of these elements provides a reader with an abundance of clues to the major themes and plot of the work.

Art, music, and literature all interact in ways that contain many opportunities for the enrichment of all of the arts. Students could apply their knowledge of art and music by creating illustrations for a work or creating a musical score for a text. Students could discuss the meanings of texts and decide on their illustrations, or a score could amplify the meaning of the text.

Understanding the art and music of a period can make the experience of literature a richer, more rewarding experience. Students should be encouraged to use the knowledge of art and music to illuminate the text. Examining examples of dress, architecture, music, and dance of a period may be helpful in a fuller engagement of the text. Much of period literature lends itself to the analysis of the prevailing taste in art and music of an era, which helps place the literary work in a more meaningful context.

Informational Sources

Informational sources often come in short forms like a memo or recipe, or longer forms like books, magazines, or journals. These longer sources of information each have their own way of organizing information, but there are some similarities that the reader should be aware of.

Most books, magazines, and journals have a **table of contents** at the beginning. This helps the reader find the different parts of the book. The table of contents is usually found a page or two after the title page in a book, and on the first few pages of a magazine. However, many magazines now place the table of contents in the midst of an overabundance of advertisements, because they know readers will have to look at the ads as they search for the table. The standard orientation for a table of contents is the sections of the book listed along the left side, with the initial page number for each along the right. It is common in a book for the prefatory material (preface, introduction, etc.) to be numbered with Roman numerals. The contents are always listed in order from the beginning of the book to the end.

A nonfiction book will also typically have an **index** at the end so that the reader can easily find information about particular topics. An index lists the topics in alphabetical order. The names of people are listed with the last name first. For example, *Adams, John* would come before *Washington, George*. To the right of the entry, the relevant page numbers are listed. When a topic is mentioned over several pages, the index will often connect these pages with a dash. For instance, if the subject is mentioned from pages 35 to 42 and again on 53, then the index entry will be labeled as *35-42, 53*. Some entries will have subsets, which are listed below the main entry, indented slightly, and placed in alphabetical order. This is common for subjects that are discussed frequently in the book. For instance, in a book about Elizabethan drama, William Shakespeare will likely be an important topic. Beneath Shakespeare's name in the index, there might be listings for *death of*, *dramatic works of*, *life of*, etc. These more specific entries help the reader refine his search.

Many informative texts, especially textbooks, use **headings** and **subheadings** for organization. Headings and subheadings are typically printed in larger and bolder fonts, and are often in a different color than the main body of the text. Headings may be larger than subheadings. Also, headings and subheadings are not always complete sentences. A heading announces the topic that will be addressed in the text below. Headings are meant to alert the reader to what is about to come. Subheadings announce the topics of smaller sections within the entire section indicated by the heading. For instance, the heading of a section in a science textbook might be *AMPHIBIANS*, and within that section might be subheadings for *Frogs*, *Salamanders*, and *Newts*. Readers should always pay close attention to headings and subheadings, because they prime the brain for the information that is about to be delivered, and because they make it easy to go back and find particular details in a long text.

Sources of Information

Books, journals, and magazines offer a lot of information to a reader at once. Other types of informational sources are targeted at a specific audience for a more limited purpose. One such type of informational source is the labeling of foods and medicines. The Food and Drug Administration has strict mandates for the information that must be included on these labels. For instance, a **food label** must list the corresponding food's number of calories, total fat, cholesterol, sodium, protein, and carbohydrates, among others. Also, a food label will usually contain a list of the vitamins that can be found in the product. Most importantly, a food label lists the serving size, which is the portion of the product for which the vitamin and nutrient values are true. Some food manufacturers use odd serving sizes to make it look as if a product is healthier than it is. When making a comparison, one should always calculate the amount of nutrients per unit of measure (grams or fluid ounces, for example) to account for these serving size distortions.

Medicine labels contain a wealth of information that can be used to make comparisons and informed purchases. Every medicine label must have detailed and comprehensive instructions regarding dosage, including how much and how often the medicine should be taken. A label will also include warning information, and what to do in case of overdose or adverse reaction. Medicine labels will have a complete list of ingredients, but will isolate the active ingredients, which are those that accomplish the advertised purpose of the product. Often, generic versions of a medicine have the same active ingredients as more expensive name-brand versions. Finally, a label will specify when a medication should not be taken by certain people, like the elderly or pregnant women. When comparing medicines, it is important to isolate the most crucial information: dosage schedule, active ingredients, and counter-indications.

A slightly different type of informational source is a **memo**. Memos are generally short, official messages written by and for members of the same organization. They usually contain a plan of action, a request for information on a specific topic, or a response to such a request. There is a standard format for these documents. It is typical for there to be a heading at the top indicating the author, date, and recipient. In some cases, this heading will also include the author's title and the name of his or her institution. Below this information will be the body of the memo. Many memos are organized with numbers or bullet points, which make it easier for the reader to identify key ideas.

Announcements are another type of written communication that gives information to readers. People post announcements for all sorts of occasions. Many people are familiar with notices for lost pets, yard sales, and landscaping services. In order to be effective, these announcements need to contain all of the information the reader requires to act on the message. For instance, a lost pet announcement needs to include a good description of the animal and a contact number for the owner. A yard sale notice should include the address, date, and hours of the sale, as well as a brief description of the products that will be available there. When composing an announcement, it is important to consider the perspective of the audience: what will they need to know in order to respond to the message? Although a posted announcement should try to use color and decoration to attract the eye of the passerby, it must also convey the necessary information.

Classified advertisements, or **ads**, are used to sell or buy goods, to attract business, to make romantic connections, and to do countless other things. They are an inexpensive, and sometimes free, way to make a brief pitch. Classified ads used to be found only in newspapers or special advertising circulars, but there are now many famous online listings as well. The style of these ads has remained basically the same. An ad usually begins with a word or phrase indicating what is being sold or sought. Then, the listing will give a brief description of the product or service. Because space is limited and costly in newspapers, classified ads there will often contain abbreviations for common attributes. For instance, two common abbreviations are *bk* for *black*, and *obo* for *or best offer*. Classified ads will then usually conclude by listing the price (or the amount the seeker is willing to pay), followed by contact information like a telephone number or email address.

A student must be able to find information in various sources. A **road atlas** is one such source that is designed specifically for drivers. It is a collection of maps that are useful for finding the distances between places, the correct roads and highways for reaching a given destination, and the relative positions of places in a certain geographic area. Most road atlases have a table at the beginning that illustrates the distance in miles between any two major cities. These tables are set up like a grid, with cities listed along the left and top sides. To find the distance between two places, follow the row of the first place perpendicular from the left until it intersects with the column of the second place. Some atlases have similar tables indicating the estimated travel time from one location to another.

Almost all maps contain a key, or legend, that defines the symbols used on the map for various landmarks. This key is usually placed in a corner of the map. It should contain listings for all of the important symbols on the map. Of course, these symbols will vary depending on the nature of the map. A road map uses different colored lines to indicate roads, highways, and interstates. A legend might also indicate the different dots and squares that are used to indicate towns of various sizes. The legend may contain information about the map's scale, though this may be elsewhere on the map. Many legends will contain special symbols, such as a picnic table indicating a campground.

Another source of information is the **card catalog**. Although rarely seen in the physical world anymore, card catalogs they still exist in most libraries in an online, digital format. These catalogs contain a wealth of information about the contents of the library. A typical card catalog entry contains the title, name of the author, year of publication, publisher, number of pages, and reference number in the Library of Congress. Most importantly, perhaps, card catalogs contain a brief summary of the book, so that a potential reader or researcher can get an idea of its contents. Many online card catalogs allow easy navigation to books on the same subject, by the same author, or close by on the library shelves. In any case, the card catalog entry will contain the library call number so that the researcher can find the book.

An **owner's manual** is the appropriate source of information for a purchased product. An owner's manual is mainly devoted to the operation and maintenance of the product. It will often begin with a brief outline of the product's parts and method of operation. Most manuals will contain the products specifications: that is, the precise details about its components and features. For the most part, though, the owner's manual will be devoted to the routine repairs and care that a non-expert owner can be expected to provide. In the owner's manual for a car, for instance, there will be instructions for tasks like changing the oil, replacing windshield wipers, and presetting stations on the radio. An owner's manual is unlikely to contain instructions for complex repairs that require special equipment. Finally, the owner's manual will often detail the service warranty associated with the product.

The **Yellow Pages** of the phone book contain commercial listings for businesses that provide services to the general public. The listings are organized according to the type of service being offered: there are sections for florists, auto mechanics, and pizza restaurants. These categories are placed in alphabetical order, and within each category, the listings are in alphabetical order. A basic listing in the yellow pages will include the name of the business, the address, and the phone number. However, some merchants elect to pay extra and have large advertisements alongside their listing in the yellow pages. For instance, a restaurant might buy enough space to print their entire menu.

Sometimes informational and technical passages will require the reader to follow a set of directions. For many people, especially those who are tactile or visual learners, this can be a difficult process. It is important to approach a **set of directions** differently than other texts. First of all, it is a good idea to scan the directions to determine whether special equipment or preparations are needed. Sometimes in a recipe, for instance, the author fails to mention that the oven should be preheated first, and then halfway through the process, the cook is supposed to be baking. After briefly reading the directions, the reader should return to the first step. When following directions, it is appropriate to complete each step before moving on to the next. If this is not possible, it is useful at least to visualize each step before reading the next.

Reference Materials

Knowledge of reference materials such as dictionaries, encyclopedias, and manuals are vital for any reader. **Dictionaries** contain information about words. A standard dictionary entry begins with a pronunciation guide for the word. The entry will also give the word's part of speech: that is, whether it is a noun, verb, adjective, etc. A good dictionary will also include the word's origins, including the language from which it is derived and its meaning in that language. This information is known as the word's etymology.

Dictionary entries are in alphabetical order. Many words have more than one definition, in which case the definitions will be numbered. Also, if a word can be used as different parts of speech, its various definitions in those different capacities may be separated. A sample entry might look like this:

WELL: (adverb) 1. in a good way (noun) 1. a hole drilled into the earth

The correct definition of a word will vary depending on how it is used in a sentence. When looking up a word found while reading, the best way to determine the relevant definition is to substitute the dictionary's definitions for the word in the text, and select the definition that seems most appropriate.

Encyclopedias used to be the best source for general information on a range of common subjects. Many people took pride in owning a set of encyclopedias, which were often written by top researchers. Now, encyclopedias largely exist online. Although they no longer have a preeminent place in general scholarship, these digital encyclopedias now often feature audio and video clips. A good encyclopedia remains the best place to obtain basic information about a well-known topic. There are also specialty encyclopedias that cover more obscure or expert information. For instance, there are many medical encyclopedias that contain the detail and sophistication required by doctors. For a regular person researching a subject like ostriches, Pennsylvania, or the Crimean War, an encyclopedia is a good source.

A **thesaurus** is a reference book that gives synonyms of words. It is different from a dictionary because a thesaurus does not give definitions, only lists of synonyms. A thesaurus can be helpful in finding the meaning of an unfamiliar word when reading. If the meaning of a synonym is known, then the meaning of the unfamiliar word will be known.

The other time a thesaurus is helpful is when writing. Using a thesaurus helps authors to vary their word choice.

A **database** is an informational source that has a different format than a publication or a memo. They are systems for storing and organizing large amounts of information. As personal computers have become more common and accessible, databases have become ever more present. The standard layout of a database is as a grid, with labels along the left side and the top. The horizontal rows and vertical columns that make up the grid are usually numbered or lettered, so that a particular square within the database might have a name like A3 or G5. Databases are good for storing information that can be expressed succinctly. They are most commonly used to store numerical data, but they also can be used to store the answers to yes-no questions and other brief data points. Information that is ambiguous (that is, has multiple possible meanings) or difficult to express in a few words is not appropriate for a database.

Often, a reader will come across a word that he does not recognize. The reader needs to know how to identify the definition of a word from its context. This means defining a word based on the words around it and the way it is used in a sentence. For instance, consider the following sentence: *The elderly scholar spent his evenings hunched over arcane texts that few other people even knew existed.* The adjective *arcane* is uncommon, but the reader can obtain significant information about it based on its use here. Based on the fact that few other people know of their existence, the reader can assume that arcane texts must be rare and only of interest to a few people. And, because they are being read by an elderly scholar, the reader can assume that they focus on difficult academic subjects. Sometimes, words can even be defined by what they are not. For instance, consider the following sentence: *Ron's fealty to his parents was not shared by Karen, who disobeyed their every command.* Because someone who disobeys is not demonstrating *fealty*, the word can be inferred to mean something like obedience or respect.

When conducting research, it is important to depend on reputable **primary sources**. A primary source is the documentary evidence closest to the subject being studied. For instance, the primary sources for an essay about penguins would be photographs and recordings of the birds, as well as accounts of people who have studied penguins in person. A secondary source would be a review of a movie about penguins or a book outlining the observations made by others. A primary source should be credible and, if it is on a subject that is still being explored, recent. One way to assess the credibility of a work is to see how often it is mentioned in other books and articles on the same subject. Just by reading the works cited and bibliographies of other books, one can get a sense of what are the acknowledged authorities in the field.

The Internet was once considered a poor place to find sources for an essay or article, but its credibility has improved greatly over the years. Still, students need to exercise caution when performing research online. The best sources are those affiliated with established institutions, like universities, public libraries, and think tanks. Most newspapers are available online, and many of them allow the public to browse their archives. Magazines frequently offer similar services. When obtaining information from an unknown website, however, one must exercise considerably more caution. A website can be considered trustworthy if it is referenced by other sites that are known to be reputable. Also, credible sites tend to be properly maintained and frequently updated. A site is easier to trust when the author provides some information about him or herself, including some credentials that indicate expertise in the subject matter.

The Writing Section

A topic will be presented to you and you must write out a discussion on it within the time allowed. There is not a "correct" answer to the topic. You must evaluate the topic, organize your ideas, and develop them into a cohesive and coherent response.

You will be scored on how well you are able to utilize standard written English, organize and explain your thoughts, and support those thoughts with reasons and examples.

Brainstorm

Spend the first few minutes brainstorming out ideas. Write down any ideas you might have on the topic. The purpose is to extract from the recesses of your memory any relevant information. In this stage, anything goes down. Write down any idea, regardless of how good it may initially seem. You can use either the scratch paper provided or the word processor to quickly jot down your thoughts and ideas. The word processor is highly recommended though, particularly if you are a fast typist.

Strength through Diversity

The best papers will contain diversity of examples and reasoning. As you brainstorm consider different perspectives. Not only are there two sides to every issue, but there are also countless perspectives that can be considered. On any issue, different groups are impacted, with many reaching the same conclusion or position, but through vastly different paths. Try to "see" the issue through as many different eyes as you can. Look at it from every angle and from every vantage point. The more diverse the reasoning used, the more balanced the paper will become and the better the score.

Example:

The issue of free trade is not just two sided. It impacts politicians, domestic (US) manufacturers, foreign manufacturers, the US economy, the world economy, strategic alliances, retailers, wholesalers, consumers, unions, workers, and the exchange of more than just goods, but also of ideas, beliefs, and cultures. The more of these angles that you can approach the issue from, the more solid your reasoning and the stronger your position.

Furthermore, don't just use information as to how the issue impacts other people. Draw liberally from your own experience and your own observations. Explain a personal experience that you have had and your own emotions from that moment. Anything that you've seen in your community or observed in society can be expanded upon to further round out your position on the issue.

Pick a Main Idea

Once you have finished with your creative flow, stop and review it. Which idea were you able to come up with the most supporting information? It's extremely important that you pick an angle that will allow you to have a thorough and comprehensive coverage of the topic. This is not about your personal convictions, but about writing a concise rational discussion of an idea.

Weed the Garden

Every garden of ideas gets weeds in it. The ideas that you brainstormed over are going to be random pieces of information of mixed value. Go through it methodically and pick out the ones that are the best. The best ideas are strong points that it will be easy to write a few sentences or a paragraph about.

Create a Logical Flow

Now that you know which ideas you are going to use and focus upon, organize them. Put your writing points in a logical order. You have your main ideas that you will focus on, and must align them in a sequence that will flow in a smooth, sensible path from point to point, so that the reader will go smoothly from one idea to the next in a logical path. Readers must have a sense of continuity as they read your paper. You don't want to have a paper that rambles back and forth.

Start Your Engines

You have a logical flow of main ideas with which to start writing. Begin expanding on the issues in the sequence that you have set for yourself. Pace yourself. Don't spend too much time on any one of the ideas that you are expanding upon. You want to have time for all of them. Make sure you watch your time. If you have ten minutes left to write out your ideas and you have ten ideas, then you can only use one minute per idea. It can be a daunting task to cram a lot of information down in words in a short amount of time, but if you pace yourself, you can get through it all. If you find that you are falling behind, speed up. Move through each idea more quickly, spending less time to expand upon the idea in order to catch back up.

Once you finish expanding on each idea, go back to where you had written out your ideas in your brainstorming session. Cross out the ideas as you write about them. This will let you see what you need to write about next, and also allow you to pace yourself and see what you have left to cover.

First Paragraph

Your first paragraph should have several easily identifiable features.

First, it should have a quick description or paraphrasing of the topic. Use your own words to briefly explain what the topic is about.

Second, you should explain your opinion of the topic and give an explanation of why you feel that way. What is your decision or conclusion on the topic?

Third, you should list your "writing points". What are the main ideas that you came up with earlier? This is your opportunity to outline the rest of your paper. Have a sentence explaining each idea that you will go intend further depth in additional paragraphs. If someone was to only read this paragraph, they should be able to get an "executive summary" of the entire paper.

Body Paragraph

Each of your successive paragraphs should expand upon one of the points listed in the main paragraph. Use your personal experience and knowledge to support each of your points. Examples should back up everything.

Conclusion Paragraph

Once you have finished expanding upon each of your main points, wrap it up. Summarize what you have said and covered in a conclusion paragraph. Explain once more your opinion of the topic and quickly review why you feel that way. At this stage, you have already backed up your statements, so there is no need to do that again. All you are doing is refreshing in the mind of the reader the main points that you have made.

Don't Panic

Panicking will not put down any more words on paper for you. Therefore, it isn't helpful. When you first see the topic, if your mind goes as blank as the page on which you have to type out your paper, take a deep breath. Force yourself to mechanically go through the steps listed above.

Secondly, don't get clock fever. It's easy to be overwhelmed when you're looking at a page that doesn't seem to have much text, there is a lot of blank space further down, your mind is full of random thoughts and feeling confused, and the clock is ticking down faster than you would like. You brainstormed first so that you don't have to keep coming up with ideas. If you're running out of time and you have a lot of ideas that you haven't expanded upon, don't be afraid to make some cuts. Start picking the best ideas that you have left and expand on those few. Don't feel like you have to write down and expand all of your ideas.

Check Your Work

It is more important to have a shorter paper that is well written and well organized, than a longer paper that is poorly written and poorly organized. Don't keep writing about a subject just to add words and sentences, and certainly don't start repeating yourself.

Expand on the ideas that you identified in the brainstorming session and make sure that you save yourself a few minutes at the end to go back and check your work.

Leave time at the end, at least a few minutes, to go back and check over your work. Reread and make sure that everything you've written makes sense and flows. Clean up any spelling or grammar mistakes that you might have made.

As you proofread, make sure there aren't any fragments or run-ons. Check for sentences that are too short or too long. If the sentence is too short, look to see if you have an identifiable subject and verb. If it is too long, break it up into two separate sentences. Watch out for any "big" words you may have used. It's good to use difficult vocabulary words, but only if you are positive that you are using them correctly. Your paper has to be correct, it doesn't have to be fancy. You're not trying to impress anyone with your vocabulary, just your ability to develop and express ideas.

Final Note

Depending on your test taking preferences and personality, the essay writing will probably be your hardest or your easiest section. You are required to go through the entire process of writing a paper in a brief amount of time, which can be quite a challenge.

Focus upon each of the steps listed above. Go through the process of creative flow first, generating ideas and thoughts about the topic. Then organize those ideas into a smooth logical flow. Pick out the ones that are best from the list you have created. Decide which main idea or angle of the topic you will discuss.

Create a recognizable structure in your paper, with an introductory paragraph explaining what you have decided upon, and what your main points will be. Use the body paragraphs to expand on those main points and have a conclusion that wraps up the issue or topic.

Save a few moments to go back and review what you have written. Clean up any minor mistakes that you might have had and give it those last few critical touches that can make a huge difference. Finally, be proud and confident of what you have written!

Special Report: How Schools View Your TOEFL Score, and What This Means for You

For your computer based TOEFL score, universities will group you in one of six categories.

Score	Policy
280 or more	admission definite for graduate students
250-279	admission definite for undergraduate students
213-249	admission likely for graduate students
173-212	admission likely for undergraduate students
133-172	individual cases reviewed
132 or less	likely referral to English language program

If you are on the upper edge of one of these categories, it is definitely profitable to work your way into the next one by studying and practicing.

Appendix A: Paper Based TOEFL/Computer Based TOEFL Equivalency Table

If you've taken the paper based TOEFL in the past and wonder what that would equate to on the computer based TOEFL, here is a table showing the equivalent scores.

Computer Based	Paper Based
284 - 300	658 - 677
271 - 283	638 - 657
261 - 270	618 - 637
248 - 260	598 - 617
234 - 247	578 - 597
221 - 233	558 - 577
204 - 220	538 - 557
188 - 203	518 - 537
171 - 187	498 - 517
154 - 170	478 - 497
138 - 153	458 - 477
124 - 137	438 - 457
108 - 123	418 - 437
94 - 107	398 - 417
81 - 93	378 - 397
71 - 80	358 - 377
58 - 70	338 - 357
48 - 57	318 - 337
40 - 47	310 - 317

Appendix B: Common Idioms and Expressions

Here is a list of the most common idioms that you could expect to encounter on the Listening Section.

ace: make an "A" on a test, homework assignment, project, etc.

"Somebody said you aced the test, Dave. That's great!"

all right (1): expression of reluctant agreement.

A: "Come to the party with me. Please!"
B: "Oh, **all right**. I don't want to, but I will."

all right (2): fair; not particularly good.

A: "How's your chemistry class?"
B: "It's **all right**, I guess, but it's not the best class I've ever had."

all right (3): unharmed; in satisfactory condition.

A: "You don't look normal. Are you **all right**?"
B: "Yes, but I have a headache."

and then some: and much more besides.

A: "I'd guess your new computer cost about $2,000. "
B: "It cost that much **and then some** because I also bought extra RAM and VRAM."

antsy: restless; impatient and tired of waiting.

"I hope Katy calls soon. Just sitting around and waiting is making me **antsy**."

as easy as pie: very easy.

"I thought you said this was a difficult problem. It isn't. In fact, it's **as easy as pie**."

at the eleventh hour: at the last minute; almost too late.

"Yes, I got the work done in time. I finished it **at the eleventh hour**, but I wasn't late."

bad-mouth: say unkind, unflattering, embarrassing (and probably untrue) things about someone.

A: "I don't believe what Bob said. Why is he bad-mouthing me?"
B: "He's probably jealous of your success."

be a piece of cake: be very easy.

A: "Bob said the test was difficult, but I thought it was **a piece of cake**.""

be all ears: be eager to hear what someone has to say.

A: "I just got an e-mail message from our old friend Sally."
B: "Tell me what she said. I'**m all ears**!"

be broke: be without money.

"No, I can't lend you ten dollars. I'**m** completely **broke** until payday."

be fed up with (with someone or something): be out of patience (with someone or something);
be very tired of someone or something.

"Bill, you're too careless with your work. I'**m fed up with**
apologizing for your mistakes!"

be in and out: be at and away from a place during a particular time.

"Could we postpone our meeting until tomorrow? I expect to
be in and out of the office most of the day today."

be on the go: be very busy (going from one thing or project to another).

"I'm really tired. I've **been on the go** all week long."

be on the road: be traveling.

"You won't be able to contact me tomorrow because I'll **be on the road**."

be over: be finished; end.

"I can't see you until around 4 o'clock. My meetings won't **be over** until then."

be up and running: (for a technological process) be operational; be ready to use .

"Dave's ESL Cafe on the Web has **been up and running** since December 1995."

be used to (+Ving/noun): be accustomed to; not uncomfortable with.

"It won't be hard to get up at 5:00 AM. I**'m used to** getting up early."

beat: exhausted; very tired (adj.).

"This has been a long day. I'm **beat**!"

beat around the bush: evade an issue; avoid giving a direct answer.

"Quit **beating around the bush**! If you don't want to go with me, just tell me!"

beat one's brains out: try very hard to understand or do something.

"Can you help me with this problem? I've been **beating my brains out** with it, but I just can't solve it."

Beats me: I have no idea.

A: "What time's the party?"
B: "**Beats me**!"

before long: soon.

A: "I'm really tired of working."
B: "Just be patient. The weekend will be here **before long**."

bent out of shape: needlessly worried about something.

"I know you're worried about your job interview, but don't get **bent out of shape**. You'll do just fine."

bite off more than one can chew: take responsibility for more than one can manage.

"I'm really behind with my project. Can you help me? I'm afraid I **bit off more than I could chew**!"

blabbermouth: a very talkative person--especially one who says things that should be kept secret.

"Don't say anything to Bob unless you want the whole office to know. Bob's quite a **blabbermouth**."

blow one's top: become extremely angry.

A: "Was your father upset when you came home at 3 AM?"
B: "He was *more than* upset. He **blew his top**!"

boom box: portable cassette/CD player.

"Don't forget to bring your **boom box** to the picnic!"

the bottom line: the most essential information.

"The discussion lasted many hours. **The bottom line** was that the XYZ Company isn't for sale."

Break a leg!: Good luck!

"I understand you have a job interview tomorrow. **Break a leg**!"

break someone's heart: make someone feel very disappointed/discouraged/sad.

"Joe **broke his mother's heart** when he dropped out of school."

broke: without money.

A: "Can you lend me 10 dollars?"
B: "I'm afraid not. I'm **broke**."

buck(s): dollar(s).

"The cheapest tickets for the concert cost 25 **bucks**. Do you still want to go?"

bug: annoy; bother.

"I'm trying to concentrate! Don't **bug** me!"

bull-headed: stubborn; inflexible.

"Don't be so **bull-headed**. Why can't you admit that others' opinions are just as good as yours?"

a bundle: a lot of money.

A: "Your new car is really nice."
B: "It should be. It cost me **a bundle**!"

burn the midnight oil: study/work all night or until very, very late at night.

"I'm not ready for the test tomorrow. I guess I'll have to
burn the the midnight oil."

bushed: very tired; exhausted.

"I'm going to lie down for a while. I'm really **bushed**."

- 54 -

by oneself: alone and without help.

"I can't do this **by myself**. Can you help me?"

by the skin of one's teeth: barely succeed in doing something.

"I'll have to start earlier the next time. This time I only finished **by the skin of my teeth**."

call it a day: stop work for the day.

"It's late and you've accomplished a lot. Why don't you **call it a day**?"

can't make heads or tails of something: can't understand something at all; find something confusing and illogical.

"I **can't make heads or tails of** your e-mail. Were you having problems with your computer?"

catch one's eye: attract one's attention/interest.

"This brochure about Tahiti **caught my eye** when I was at the travel agency."

catch some Zs: sleep for a while; take a nap.

"You look tired, Dave. Why don't you **catch some Zs**?"

change one's mind: decide to do something different from what had been decided earlier.

A: "Why are you working this week? I thought you were going to be on vacation."
B: "I changed my mind. I'm taking my vacation next month."

chicken (adjective or noun): cowardly.

"Fred will never ask Lucy for a date. He's **chicken / a chicken**.

chow: food.

"How's the **chow** in the university cafeteria?"

chow down: eat.

"It's almost 6:00. Are you ready to **chow down**?"

a cinch: something that's very easy to do.

A: How was the test?
B: It was **a cinch**. I finished it quickly and I know that all my answers were correct."

cool (also *kewl*): neat, special, wonderful.

"The ESL Cafe on the Web is really **cool**!"

Cool it!: calm down.

"There's no need to be so upset. Just **cool it**!"

cost (someone) an arm and a leg: cost a lot; be very expensive.

A: "Your new car is really nice."
B: "It should be. It **cost (me) an arm and a leg**!"

couch potato: someone who spends too much time watching TV.

"You're a real **couch potato**, Jay. You need to get more exercise!"

cram: try to learn as much as possible in a very short time.

"Sidney did well on the test because he crammed for it. However, he probably won't remember any of the information a couple of days from now."

crash course: short course designed to give a lot of knowledge/information in a very short time.

"Tom's company is sending him to a business meeting in Istanbul.

Should he take a **crash course** in Turkish?"

Cut it out!: stop doing something (that's annoying).

"You kids are making too much noise. **Cut it out**!"

Don't count your chickens until (before) they hatch (they've hatched).: Don't assume that something will happen until it *has* happened.

A: I'm sure that I'm going to win a lot of money in Las Vegas."
B: "**Don't count your chickens until they hatch**!"

dicey: uncertain; taking too much of a chance.

A: A friend of mine says I can make a lot of moneyif I buy stock
in the XYZ company. Should I do it?

B: I wouldn't if I were you. The chances for success are too **dicey**."

ditch class: skip class/play hookey.

"You shouldn't have **ditched class** yesterday. We had an unannounced test."

do a bang-up job: do a very good job; do very well at something.

"Have you seen Frank's home page? He **did a bang-up job** with it."

down in the dumps: depressed; "blue."

A: "Is something wrong?"
B: "Not really, but I feel kind of **down in the dumps**."

drop someone a line: write to someone.

"I haven't written to my parents for a long time. I'd better **drop them a line**
today or tomorrow."

drag one's feet: delay; take longer than necessary to do something.

"Joe should have finished his project a week ago. Why is he **dragging his feet**?"

an eager beaver: a person who is always willing to volunteer or do extra work.

"Jan is certainly **an eager beaver**. Any time there's work to be done, she's the first to say she'll help."

Easy does it!: Be very careful! / Don't do anything too fast or too hard!

A: "I'm going to move the table just a little further from the window."
B: "**Easy does it**! If you move too fast, you might knock over the plant!"

an egghead: a very intelligent person.

"Jake didn't make very good grades in school, but his sister was a real **egghead**."

elbow grease: hard work; effort.

"Yes, the car is pretty dirty, but it'll look nice again with a little **elbow grease**."

every other ____ : alternately; omitting the second one in each group of two.

"In your essays, please write on **every other line**. That will make the essays much easier to read."

far-fetched: difficult to accept; difficult to believe.

"That story's pretty **far-fetched**. Nobody's going to believe it."

feel blue: feel sad and depressed.

"I'm **feeling blue** because I haven't had any mail except bills for a long, long time."

fire someone: dismiss someone from a job because of poor performance.

"If you continue to be late for work, the company will **fire you**."

feel puny: feel unwell, ill.

"Ted was **feeling puny** yesterday, so he decided not to go to work."

fender-bender: automobile accident.

"Traffic was really slow on the freeway this morning
because of a **fender-bender** in one of the westbound lanes."

for ages: for a very long time.

"Where's Marie? I haven't seen her **for ages**."

get going: leave.

"Look at the time! I'd better **get going**!"

get it: understand something (often negative).

"I don't **get it**. What do you mean?"

get a kick out of something: find something amusing.

"I really **get a kick out of** listening to children talk. They say some very funny things."

get lost!: go away

"I wish he'd **get lost** and stop bothering me. I don't want to talk to him!"

get on one's nerves: irritate someone; make someone upset.

"I know you like that song, but it's **getting on my nerves**. Can you play something else?"

get a move on: hurry

"If you don't want to be late, you'd better **get a move on**."

get one's wires crossed: be confused or mistaken about something.

A: "Bill said there was a meeting this morning. Don't we have one?"
B: "No. The meeting's tomorrow. I guess Bill **got his wires crossed**."

get out of hand: become out of control; become badly managed.

"Your absences are **getting out of hand**, Bob. You'd better do something quickly to improve the situation if you want to keep your job."

Get real!: Be realistic! / Don't be naive.

A: "I'm going to Las Vegas. I know I'll win a lot of money!"
B: "Get real! You'll probably *lose* a lot of money!"

get up and go: energy.

"I'm really tired. I don't have any **get up and go**."

give someone a hand (1): help someone.

"I can't do this alone. Can you **give me a hand**?"

give someone a hand (2): applaud (to show respect or appreciation for someone/something).

"Dave's done a wonderful job with The ESL Café on the Web.
Let's **give him a hand**!"

a (real) go-getter: a (very) ambitious, hard-working person.

"I'm not surprised that Jean finished before anyone else. She's **a real go-getter**."

go with the flow: take things as they come.

- 60 -

"There's no need to worry. Everything will be OK if you just **go with the flow**."

grab a bite: get something to eat.

"I'm really hungry. Would you like to **grab a bite** with me?"

green: inexperienced.

"I don't think you can depend on Jack to do that job by himself. He's too **green**."

had ('d) better: be obliged to; should (strong).

"You'**d better** leave soon. If you don't, you'll miss your bus."

hassle (noun): a troublesome situation; something troublesome that interrupts one's normal routine.

"I know it's **a hassle** to complete this form now, but Mr. Rogers
needs it in his office by the end of the day."

hard feelings: anger; animosity; bitter feelings.

A: "I'm sorry that Jim got the job instead of you."
B: "I have no **hard feelings** toward him; I know that he had stronger qualifications."

hard-headed: stubborn; inflexible; unwilling to change.

"I don't think Julie will change her mind. She's pretty **hard-headed**."

hassle (verb): annoy; bother; interrupt one's normal routine.

"If you'd stop **hassling** me, I might get this finished on time!"

have one's hands full: be extremely busy.

A: "Will you be able to help us this afternoon?"

B: "I'm afraid not. I'll **have my hands full** trying to finish my research paper."

have/has ('ve/'s) got: have/has.

"Dave**'s got** a son whose name is Benjamin and a daughter whose name is Shannon."

have something down pat: know/understand something completely and thoroughly.

"I know I did well on the test. I **had** all the material **down pat**."

head honcho: person in charge; top boss.

"Dave's the **head honcho** of the ESL Cafe on the Web."

hit the books: study.

"I wish I could go to the movies, but I've got to **hit the books**."

hit the hay: go to bed; go to sleep.

"It's late, so I guess I'll **hit the hay**."

hit the sack: go to bed.

"I'm really tired. I think I'll **hit the sack**."

How come?: Why? (statement word order).

"**How come** you weren't at the party?"

if I had my druthers: if I could do what I wanted/preferred.

"**If I had my druthers**, I'd stay home from work today."

in over one's head: in a situation that is too much / too difficult for one to manage.

"Do you have time to help me? I thought I could do this myself, but I'm afraid I'm **in over my head**. I just can't handle things alone."

inside out: with the inner part on the outside and the outer part on the inside.

"Why are you wearing your tee shirt **inside out**?"

in stock: in supply and available to buy / sell.

"I'm sorry, but we just sold our last pair of hiking boots. If you come back at the end of the week, however, we should have some more **in stock**.

in the black: profitable; not showing a financial loss.

"What did you do to increase profit and eliminate losses? We've been **in the black** for two months in a row."

in the red: unprofitable; showing a financial loss.

"We have to do something to increase profit and decrease losses. We've been **in the red** for two months in a row."

in time: not late.

"I thought I was going to be late for my flight, but it was delayed, so I was still **in time**."

jump all over someone: severely criticize / find fault with someone.

A: "What's wrong with Joe?"
B: "He's feeling bad because his boss **jumped all over him** this morning."

jump the gun: do something before it's time to do it.

A: "How did Marsha know about the party? It was supposed to be a surprise."

B: "Chuck **jumped the gun**. Without thinking, he said, 'I'm bringing the cake at your party; I hope you like it!"

jump to conclusions: decide something too quickly and without thinking about it or considering all the facts.

A: "Angela just doesn't like me. She won't even say hello."
B: "You're **jumping to conclusions**. Actually, she's very shy."

junk mail: unsolicited mail (usually advertisements for something you're not interested in).

"I didn't have any letters today--only **junk mail**."

keep an eye on: check something regularly.

"You're busy, so you'll need to **keep an eye on** the time.
Remember that we have to leave at 4:30."

keep an eye out for: watch for.

"I'll **keep an eye out for** John. If I see him, I'll tell him you want to talk to him."

keep one's chin up: remain brave and confident in a difficult situation;
don't despair or worry too much.

"I know that things have been difficult for you recently,
but **keep your chin up**. Everything will be better soon."

keep one's nose to the grindstone: stay diligent; steadily work hard,
without breaks or an uneven pace.

"If I **keep my nose to the grindstone**, I should be finished by the end of the day."

keep/stay in touch (with someone): remain informed (about someone) / in contact (with someone) by writing, calling, sending e-mail, etc. on a regular basis.

"I haven't seen Frank for two or three years but we **keep** (stay) **in touch** by e-mail."

keep one's fingers crossed: hope for the best.

A: "How did you do on the test?"

B: "I think I passed, but I won't know until tomorrow.
I'm **keeping my fingers crossed**!"

kid (noun): child.

A: "You have three **kids**, don't you?"
B: "That's right. I have two girls and a boy."

kid (verb): playfully say something that isn't true.

"I was **kidding** when I said my teacher was a monster. She's strict,
but she's actually a very nice person."

kind of: rather; more or less; a little.

"I'm feeling **kind of** hungry. I think I'll make myself a sandwich."

a klutz: an awkward, uncoordinated person.

"Don't ask Jeff to dance with you. He's a real **klutz** and will probably step on your feet!"

a know-it-all: someone who acts as if he/she knows everything--as if no one
can tell him/her anything that he/she doesn't already know.

"Don't try to make any suggestions to Bob. He's **a know-it-all**
and won't pay attention to anything you say."

know something backwards and forwards: know/understand something
completely and thoroughly.

"If you have a question about html tags, ask Susan. She knows html
backwards and forwards."

know something inside out: know/understand something thoroughly.

"If you have a question about grammar, ask Dr. Martin. She **knows** grammar **inside out**."

lend someone a hand: help someone.

"I can't do this alone. Can you **lend me a hand**?"

leave well enough alone: do nothing (because doing something would make things worse).

"Don't tell Jim how to discipline his children. **Leave well enough alone**."

a let-down: a disappointment; something that's very disappointing.

"It must've been quite a **let-down** not to be chosen for that job.
I know you really hoped you would get it."

Let sleeping dogs lie.: Don't cause problems by doing something when it isn't necessary.

"I know that what Julie said made you angry, but **let sleeping dogs lie**.
If you say or do anything, you'll only make things worse."

live from hand to mouth: survive on very little money; have only enough money
to pay for basic needs.

"Chuck and Alice are **living from hand to mouth** since Chuck lost his job."

live and let live: don't unnecessarily make things difficult;
do as you wish and let others do as they wish.

"I'm not going to criticize Alice's family just because their habits
are a little strange. My motto is '**Live and let live**.'"

a low blow: a big disappointment.

A: "Fred seems depressed. Is he OK?"
B: "He's OK, but not good. It was **a low blow** for him to be laid off from his job."

lousy: terrible; very bad.

"Why did you speak so rudely to your grandmother? That was a **lousy** thing to do!"

macho: super masculine / masculine to an extreme (in appearance and behavior).

"Her husband would never agree to help with the housework;
he's too **macho** to do that."

make a mountain out of a molehill: make something seem much more important than it really is.

"Calm down. There's really nothing to worry about.
You're **making a mountain out of a molehill**."

make up one's mind: decide what to do.

A: Where are you going on your vacation?
B: Maybe Canada, maybe Mexico. I can't **make up my mind**."

No way!: Absolutely not! / Definitely not!

A: "You didn't open this letter addressed to me, did you?"
B: "**No way**! I'd *never* read look at else's mail!"

nosh: snack.

"There's plenty in the refrigerator if you want something to **nosh** on."

Not on your life!: Absolutely not! (a strong "no").

A: "Someone said you cheated on the test. Did you?"
B: "**Not on your life!**"

now and then: occasionally; from time to time.

A: "Do you see Jennifer often?"
B: "No, not really. I see her **now and then**, but not regularly."

nuke: heat in a microwave.

"If your coffee's cold, just **nuke** it for about a minute."

nuts: crazy.

A: "Stuart says some really strange things sometimes."
B: "Sometimes? All the time! He's **nuts**!"

OK: (1) yes (to show agreement--often reluctant agreement).

A: "Come on, Al. We really need your help!"
B: "Oh, **OK**; I may be crazy, but I'll help you."

OK: (2) neither good nor bad; so-so.

A: "How was the movie?"
B: "**OK**, I guess, but I've seen better ones."

OK: (3) in satisfactory condition; well.

A: "You look awfully pale. Are you **OK**?"
B: "Actually, I'm not. I have a terrible headache. "

OK: (4) approve (verb).

A: "Did your boss **OK** your vacation plans?"
B: "No, but he said that taking them two weeks later would be all right.

on the dot: exactly at a given time.

"We're leaving at 9:00 **on the dot**. If you're late, we'll go without you."

on time: at the scheduled time.

"It's getting late. You'd better hurry if you want to get to work **on time**."

(on the) cutting edge: using the most recent technology.

"The university's computer lab is **(on the) cutting edge**. It has all the latest hardware and software."

once in a while: occasionally; from time to time.

A: "Would you like coffee or tea?"
B: "Coffee, please. I drink tea **once in a while**, but I generally drink coffee."

over one's head: too difficult or complicated for someone to understand.

"This explanation of cgi scripting is **over my head**.
Can you explain it in a less technical way?"

pay the piper: face the consequences for something you've done.

"I stayed up too late tonight. Tomorrow I'll have to **pay the piper**."

plastic: credit card(s).

"Oh, no! I forgot to get any cash! I hope this restaurant accepts **plastic**!"

pooped: very tired; exhausted.

"I went to bed really early last night. I was **pooped**!"

pop quiz: unannounced short test.

"You shouldn't have missed class yesterday. We had a **pop quiz**."

pretty (adv.): rather; somewhat.

"That car's **pretty** expensive. Are you sure you can afford it?"

pull an all-nighter: study or work all night without getting any sleep.

A: "You look really tired."

B: "I am. I **pulled an all-nighter** to get ready for the meeting this morning."

pull someone's leg: tease someone by trying to make her/him believe something that's exaggerated or untrue.

A: "Wow! Carl has done some really amazing things!"

B: "Don't believe everything he tells you. He was probably **pulling your leg**."

quite a few: several; numerous.

"I don't think I can meet you after work. I have **quite a few** errands that I have to do."

a quick study: someone who learns new things quickly and easily.

A: "Annie seems to be doing well at her new job."

B: "I'm not surprised. She's **a quick study**."

R and R: rest and relaxation (a vacation).

"I think you're working too hard, Dave. You need some **R and R**."

rain or shine: (describing something scheduled) no matter what the weather is.

"We're leaving tomorrow, **rain or shine**."

rain cats and dogs: rain very hard.

"You can't leave just now! It's **raining cats and dogs**
and you don't have an umbrella or raincoat!"

read someone's mind: know what someone is thinking.

A: "I'll be you're thinking of what you're going to have for dinner."

B: "Hey, did you **read my mind**?"

A: "No. I just know that you're always hungry and lunch was several hours ago!"

rub someone the wrong way: irritate someone; bother or annoy someone.

"All my little brother says is 'Why?' Usually I'm patient with him,
but sometimes all his questions **rub me the wrong way**."

run-down: (1) not well; weak; fatigued.

"Are you eating regularly and getting enough sleep? You look **run-down**."

run-down: (2) in poor condition; needing repair.

"This must be a poor neighborhood. All the buildings look really **run-down**."

__ **-savvy:** knowledgeable about __ .

"If you're having problems with your hard disk, talk to Jim.
He's very **computer-savvy**. "

schmooze: make relaxed, casual conversation.

"No, we weren't talking about anything important.
We were just **schmoozing**."

shoot the breeze: make relaxed, casual conversation.

"No, we weren't talking about anything important.
We were just **shooting the breeze**."

sleep on it: take at least a day to think about something before making a decision.

"The job that you're offering me sounds really good, but I'd like
to **sleep on it** before giving you my final decision."

a snap: something that's very easy to do.

A: "Is your job difficult?"

B: "No, actually it's **a snap**. In fact, it's so easy that it's a little bit boring."

Someone's made his/her own bed; now let him/her lie in it.: Someone has caused his/her own problems; he/she will have to solve them himself/herself.

A: Jim upset everyone when he got angry at the meeting. Can we do anything to make the situation better?

B: No. **He's made his own bed; now let him lie in it.**"

sooner or later: eventually.

"You've been working too hard for too long. If you don't relax a little, **sooner or later** you're going to get sick."

sort of: rather; somewhat.

"I think I'll lie down. I feel **sort of** dizzy."

so-so: fair; not particularly good.

A: "How're you doing?"
B: "**So-so**. I've been better, but I've also been worse."

state of the art: using the latest technology.

"The company is very proud of the equipment in its computer room. It's **state of the art**."

Step on it!: Hurry up!

"**Step on it**! The taxi will be here at any time and you're not even dressed!"

take it easy: relax.

"I don't have any special vacation plans. I'm just going to **take it easy**."

tell a white lie: say something that isn't true in order not to hurt or offend someone.

"The cake that Susan made tasted terrible, but I knew that she
made it because she wanted to please me, so when she asked
if I liked it, I **told a white lie** and said it was good."

toss something: throw something away; put something in the trash.

"These shoes are worn out. I guess I'll have to **toss them**."

tough: difficult.

"Question number three is a **tough** one.Do you know the answer?"

There, there.: expression of comfort.

"**There, there**. Everything's going to be OK."

tight-fisted: very frugal; unwilling to spend money unnecessarily.

A: Do you think Charlie will donate any money to the activities fund?
B: No way! He's too **tight-fisted**!

a tightwad: someone who is very frugal and unwilling to spend money unnecessarily.

A: Will Charlie donate any money to the activities fund?
B: Absolutely not! He's a real **tightwad**!"

tricky: easily confused or misunderstood.

"This problem is **tricky**. I don't really understand it."

two-faced: deceitful; disolyal; someone who pretends to be a friend but isn't.

"I thought he was my friend, but he's **two-faced**. He says nice things
to me when we're together, but makes jokes about me when we aren't.

under the weather: ill; sick; unwell.

"Ted was feeling **under the weather** yesterday, so he decided not to go to work."

until hell freezes over: forever.

"Chris can practice the piano **until hell freezes over**, but he'll never play well because he's tone-deaf."

Note: This expression is used to describe something that will not change, no matter how long or how often it's done.

until you're blue in the face: forever.

"You can talk **until you're blue in the face**, but I won't change my mind."

Note: This expression is used in the same way as "until hell freezes over."

update: make current; add information to show what has happened recently.

"I need to **update** my résumé. It doesn't show what I've done during the last year."

upside down: with the bottom part on top and the top part on bottom.

"Put the glasses **upside down** in the dishwasher. If you don't do that, they'll fill with water and you'll have to dry them by hand."

used to (+ V): an action that was true in the past but is not true now.

"Jane **used to** live in Austin, Texas. She lives in San Francisco now."

Was my face red!: I was very embarrassed.

"When I got to the meeting I noticed that I was wearing one black sock and one brown one. **Was my face red!**"

wear out one's welcome: make someone uncomfortable by visiting too long.

A: "Can't you stay two or three more days?"
B: "No. I don't want to **wear out my welcome**."

wet behind the ears: inexperienced and naive.

"Don't include Fred as part of the bargaining team.He's just started working here and is still too **wet behind the ears**."

What for?: Why?

A: "Come here for a minute. I need you."
B: "What for?"

Note: "What" and "for" can be separated--with "for" at the end of the question:

B: "What do you need me for?"

What's up?: What's new? What's happening?

"Hi, Dave. **What's up**?"

a white lie: a lie that is told to avoid offending someone or hurting his / her feelings.

"The cake that Susan made tasted terrible, but I knew that she made it because she wanted to please me, so when she asked if I liked it, I told a white lie and said it was good."

wishy-washy: uncommitted; without an opinion of one's own.

"Don't be so **wishy-washy**. Tell us how you really feel."

with bells on: very eagerly; with the feeling that one will have a very good time.

A: "Are you going to Sandra's party?"
B: "I'll be there **with bells on**!"

would ('d) just as soon: would ('d) rather; prefer.

"I know we have a lot of work to do, but I'm tired. I**'d just as soon** leave and finish tomorrow. Is that OK with you?"

a yes-man: someone who tries to get approval by agreeing with everyone.

A: "Why does the boss think Arnold is so intelligent?"
B: "Because Arnold is **a yes-man**. He agrees with everything the boss says!"

You don't say!: Really? / Is that really true?

A: "Have you heard the news? Jessica got married!"
B: "**You don't say!**"

You've got to be kidding!: You can't be serious! (What you said can't be true. What you said is very surprising/hard to believe.) "

A: "Did you know that Bob quit his job?"
B: "**You've got to be kidding!**"

yucky: terrible; distasteful; very unpleasant.

"Don't eat the soup at the cafeteria. It's **yucky**!"

yummy: delicious.

"Have you tried the cookies that Jonathan baked? They're **yummy**!"

zilch: nothing.

A: "How much money do you have?"
B: "**Zilch**. I'm broke until payday."

Zip your lip!: keep something secret; promise not to tell what has just been said.

"What I told you is really important, so **zip your lip**!"

Secret Key #1 – Time is Your Greatest Enemy

To succeed on the TOEFL, you must use your time wisely. Many students do not finish at least one section. The table below shows the time challenge you are faced with:

SECTION	Total amount of time allotted	Number of questions
Reading	60-100 min	36-70
Listening	60-90 min	34-51
BREAK	10 min	N/A
Speaking	20 min	6 tasks
Writing	50 min	2 tasks

As you can see, the time constraints are brutal. To succeed, you must ration your time properly. The reason that time is so critical is that every question counts the same toward your final score. If you run out of time on any passage, the questions that you do not answer will hurt your score far more than earlier questions that you spent extra time on and feel certain are correct.

On the Reading section, the test is separated into passages. The reason that time is so critical is that 1) every question counts the same toward your final score, and 2) the passages are not in order of difficulty. If you have to rush during the last passage, then you will miss out on answering easier questions correctly. It is natural to want to pause and figure out the hardest questions, but you must resist the temptation and move quickly.

Success Strategy #1

Pace Yourself

Wear a watch to the TOEFL Test. At the beginning of the test, check the time (or start a chronometer on your watch to count the minutes), and check the time after each passage or every few questions to make sure you are "on schedule." An onscreen clock display will keep track of your remaining time, but it may be easier for you to monitor your pace based on how many minutes have been used, rather than how many minutes remain.

If you find that you are falling behind time during the test, you must speed up. Yet although a rushed answer is more likely to be incorrect, it is better to miss a couple of questions by being rushed, than to completely miss later questions by not having enough time. It is better to end with more time than you need than to run out of time.

If you are forced to speed up, do it efficiently. Usually one or more answer choices can be eliminated without too much difficulty. Above all, don't panic. Don't speed up and just begin guessing at random choices. By pacing yourself, and continually monitoring your progress against the clock or your watch, you will always know exactly how far ahead or behind you are with your available time. If you find that you are one minute behind on one of the sections, don't skip one question without spending any time on it, just to catch back up. Spend a little less time than normal on the next few questions and after a few questions, you will have caught back up more gradually. Once you catch back up, you can continue working each problem at your normal pace.

Furthermore, don't dwell on the problems that you were rushed on. If a problem was taking up too much time and you made a hurried guess, it must be difficult. The difficult questions are the ones you are most likely to miss anyway, so it isn't a big loss.
Lastly, sometimes it is beneficial to slow down if you are constantly getting ahead of time. You are always more likely to catch a careless mistake by working more slowly than quickly, and among very high-scoring test takers (those who are likely to have lots of time left over), careless errors affect the score more than mastery of material.

- 78 -

Scanning

For Reading passages, don't waste time reading, enjoying, and completely understanding the passage. Simply scan the passage to get a rough idea of what it is about. You will return to the passage for each question, so there is no need to memorize it. Only spend as much time scanning as is necessary to get a vague impression of its overall subject content.

Secret Key #2 – Guessing is Not Guesswork

You probably know that guessing is a good idea on the TOEFL- unlike other standardized tests, there is no penalty for getting a wrong answer. Even if you have no idea about a question, you still have a 20-25% chance of getting it right.

Most students do not understand the impact that proper guessing can have on their score. Unless you score extremely high, guessing will significantly contribute to your final score.

Monkeys Take the TOEFL

What most students don't realize is that to insure that 20-25% chance, you have to guess randomly. If you put 20 monkeys in a room to take the TOEFL, assuming they answered once per question and behaved themselves, on average they would get 20-25% of the questions correct. Put 20 students in the room, and the average will be much lower among guessed questions. Why?

1. TOEFL intentionally writes deceptive answer choices that "look" right. A student has no idea about a question, so picks the "best looking" answer, which is often wrong. The monkey has no idea what looks good and what doesn't, so will consistently be lucky about 20-25% of the time.
2. Test takers will eliminate answer choices from the guessing pool based on a hunch or intuition. Simple but correct answers often get excluded, leaving a 0% chance of being correct. The monkey has no clue, and often gets lucky with the best choice.

This is why the common process of elimination is flawed and detrimental to your performance- test takers don't guess, they make an ignorant stab in the dark that is usually worse than random.

Success Strategy #2

Let me introduce one of the most valuable ideas of this course- the $5 challenge:

You only mark your "best guess" if you are willing to bet $5 on it.
You only eliminate choices from guessing if you are willing to bet $5 on it.

Why $5? Five dollars is an amount of money that is small yet not insignificant, and can really add up fast (20 questions could cost you $100). Likewise, each answer choice on one question of the TOEFL will have a small impact on your overall score, but it can really add up to a lot of points in the end.

The process of elimination IS valuable. The following shows your chance of guessing it right:

If you eliminate this many choices:	0	1	2	3
Chance of getting it correct	25%	33%	50%	100%

However, if you accidentally eliminate the right answer or go on a hunch for an incorrect answer, your chances drop dramatically: to 0%. By guessing among all the answer choices, you are GUARANTEED to have a shot at the right answer.

That's why the $5 test is so valuable- if you give up the advantage and safety of a pure guess, it had better be worth the risk.

What we still haven't covered is how to be sure that whatever guess you make is truly random. Here's the easiest way:

Always pick the first answer choice among those remaining.

Such a technique means that you have decided, **before you see a single test question**, exactly how you are going to guess- and since the order of choices tells you nothing about which one is correct, this guessing technique is perfectly random.

Let's try an example-

A test taker encounters the following problem on the Reading section about the chemical term "amine," a derivative of ammonia:

In paragraph 3, the amine will be?
- A. neutralized
- B. protonated
- C. deprotonated
- D. eliminated

The student has a small idea about this question- he is pretty sure that the amine will be deprotonated, but he wouldn't bet $5 on it. He knows that the amine is either protonated or deprotoned, so he is willing to bet $5 on both choices A and D not being correct. Now he is down to B and C. At this point, he guesses B, since B is the first choice remaining.

The student is correct by choosing B, since the amine will be protonated. He only eliminated those choices he was willing to bet money on, AND he did not let his stale memories (often things not known definitely will get mixed up in the exact opposite arrangement in one's head) about protonation and deprotonation influence his guess. He blindly chose the first remaining choice, and was rewarded with the fruits of a random guess.

This section is not meant to scare you away from making educated guesses or eliminating choices- you just need to define when a choice is worth eliminating. The $5 test, along with a pre-defined random guessing strategy, is the best way to make sure you reap all of the benefits of guessing.

Specific Guessing Techniques

Slang

Scientific sounding answers are better than slang ones. In the answer choices below, choice B is much less scientific and is incorrect, while choice A is a scientific analytical choice and is correct.

Example:

A.) To compare the outcomes of the two different kinds of treatment.

B.) Because some subjects insisted on getting one or the other of the treatments.

Extreme Statements

Avoid wild answers that throw out highly controversial ideas that are proclaimed as established fact. Choice A is a radical idea and is incorrect. Choice B is a calm rational statement. Notice that Choice B does not make a definitive, uncompromising stance, using a hedge word "if" to provide wiggle room.

Example:

A.) Bypass surgery should be discontinued completely.

B.) Medication should be used instead of surgery for patients who have not had a heart attack if they suffer from mild chest pain and mild coronary artery blockage.

Similar Answer Choices

When you have two answer choices that are direct opposites, one of them is usually the correct answer.

Example:

A.) Paragraph 1 described the author's reasoning about the influence of his childhood on his adult life.

B.) Paragraph 2 described the author's reasoning about the influence of his childhood on his adult life.

These two answer choices are very similar and fall into the same family of answer choices. A family of answer choices is when two or three answer choices are very similar. Often two will be opposites and one may show an equality.

Example:

A.) Plan I or Plan II can be conducted at equal cost

B.) Plan I would be less expensive than Plan II

C.) Plan II would be less expensive than Plan I

D.) Neither Plan I nor Plan II would be effective

Note how the first three choices are all related. They all ask about a cost comparison. Beware of immediately recognizing choices B and C as opposites and choosing one of those two. Choice A is in the same family of questions and should be considered as well. However, choice D is not in the same family of questions. It has nothing to do with cost and can be discounted in most cases.

Hedging

When asked for a conclusion that may be drawn, look for critical "hedge" phrases, such as likely, may, can, will often, sometimes, etc, often, almost, mostly, usually, generally, rarely, sometimes. Question writers insert these hedge phrases to cover every possibility. Often an answer will be wrong simply because it leaves no room for exception. Avoid answer choices that have definitive words like "exactly," and "always".

Summary of Guessing Techniques

1. Eliminate as many choices as you can by using the $5 test. Use the common guessing strategies to help in the elimination process, but only eliminate choices that pass the $5 test.

2. Among the remaining choices, only pick your "best guess" if it passes the $5 test.

3. Otherwise, guess randomly by picking the first remaining choice.

Secret Key #3 – Practice Smarter, Not Harder

Many test takers delay the test preparation process because they dread the awful amounts of practice time they think necessary to succeed on the test. We have refined an effective method that will take you only a fraction of the time.

There are a number of "obstacles" in your way to succeed. Among these are answering questions, finishing in time, and mastering test-taking strategies. All must be executed on the day of the test at peak performance, or your score will suffer. The test is a mental marathon that has a large impact on your future.

Just like a marathon runner, it is important to work your way up to the full challenge. So first you just worry about questions, and then time, and finally strategy:

Success Strategy

1. Find a good source for practice tests.
2. If you are willing to make a larger time investment, consider using more than one study guide- often the different approaches of multiple authors will help you "get" difficult concepts.
3. Take a practice test with no time constraints, with all study helps "open book." Take your time with questions and focus on applying strategies.
4. Take a practice test with time constraints, with all guides "open book."
5. Take a final practice test with no open material and time limits

If you have time to take more practice tests, just repeat step 5. By gradually exposing yourself to the full rigors of the test environment, you will condition your mind to the stress of test day and maximize your success.

Secret Key #4 – Prepare, Don't Procrastinate

Let me state an obvious fact: if you take the test three times, you will get three different scores. This is due to the way you feel on test day, the level of preparedness you have, and, despite the test writers' claims to the contrary, some tests WILL be easier for you than others.

Since your future depends so much on your score, you should maximize your chances of success. In order to maximize the likelihood of success, you've got to prepare in advance. This means taking practice tests and spending time learning the information and test taking strategies you will need to succeed.

Since you have to pay a registration fee each time you take the test, don't take it as a "practice" test. Feel free to take sample tests on your own, but when you go to take the official test, be prepared, be focused, and do your best the first time!

Secret Key #5 – Test Yourself

Everyone knows that time is money. There is no need to spend too much of your time or too little of your time preparing for the test. You should only spend as much of your precious time preparing as is necessary for you to pass it.

Once you have taken a practice test under real conditions of time constraints, then you will know if you are ready for the test or not.

If you have scored extremely high the first time that you take the practice test, then there is not much point in spending countless hours studying. You are already there.

Benchmark your abilities by retaking practice tests and seeing how much you have improved. Once you score high enough to guarantee success, then you are ready.

If you have scored well below where you need, then knuckle down and begin studying in earnest. Check your improvement regularly through the use of practice tests under real conditions. Above all, don't worry, panic, or give up. The key is perseverance!

Then, when you go to take the test, remain confident and remember how well you did on the practice tests. If you can score high enough on a practice test, then you can do the same on the real thing.

General Strategies

The most important thing you can do is to ignore your fears and jump into the test immediately- do not be overwhelmed by any strange-sounding terms. You have to jump into the test like jumping into a pool- all at once is the easiest way.

Make Predictions

As you read and understand the question, try to guess what the answer will be. Remember that several of the answer choices are wrong, and once you begin reading them, your mind will immediately become cluttered with answer choices designed to throw you off. Your mind is typically the most focused immediately after you have read the question and digested its contents. If you can, try to predict what the correct answer will be. You may be surprised at what you can predict.

Quickly scan the choices and see if your prediction is in the listed answer choices. If it is, then you can be quite confident that you have the right answer. It still won't hurt to check the other answer choices, but most of the time, you've got it!

Answer the Question

It may seem obvious to only pick answer choices that answer the question, but the test writers can create some excellent answer choices that are wrong. Don't pick an answer just because it sounds right, or you believe it to be true. It MUST answer the question. Once you've made your selection, always go back and check it against the question and make sure that you didn't misread the question, and the answer choice does answer the question posed.

Benchmark

After you read the first answer choice, decide if you think it sounds correct or not. If it doesn't, move on to the next answer choice. If it does, mentally mark that answer choice. This doesn't mean that you've definitely selected it as your answer choice, it just means that it's the best you've seen thus far. Go ahead and read the next choice. If the next choice is worse than the one you've already selected, keep going to the next answer choice. If the next choice is better than the choice you've already selected, mentally mark the new answer choice as your best guess.

The first answer choice that you select becomes your standard. Every other answer choice must be benchmarked against that standard. That choice is correct until proven otherwise by another answer choice beating it out. Once you've decided that no other answer choice seems as good, do one final check to ensure that your answer choice answers the question posed.

Valid Information

Don't discount any of the information provided in the question. Every piece of information may be necessary to determine the correct answer. None of the information in the question is there to throw you off (while the answer choices will certainly have information to throw you off). If two seemingly unrelated topics are discussed, don't ignore either. You can be confident there is a relationship, or it wouldn't be included in the question, and you are probably going to have to determine what is that relationship to find the answer.

Avoid "Fact Traps"

Don't get distracted by a choice that is factually true. Your search is for the answer that answers the question. Stay focused and don't fall for an answer that is true but incorrect. Always go back to the question and make sure you're choosing an answer that actually answers the question and is not just a true statement. An answer can be factually correct, but it MUST answer the question asked. Additionally, two answers can both be seemingly correct, so be sure to read all of the answer choices, and make sure that you get the one that BEST answers the question.

Milk the Question

Some of the questions may throw you completely off. They might deal with a subject you have not been exposed to, or one that you haven't reviewed in years. While your lack of knowledge about the subject will be a hindrance, the question itself can give you many clues that will help you find the correct answer. Read the question carefully and look for clues. Watch particularly for adjectives and nouns describing difficult terms or words that you don't recognize. Regardless of if you completely understand a word or not, replacing it with a synonym either provided or one you more familiar with may help you to understand what the questions are asking. Rather than wracking your mind about specific detailed information concerning a difficult term or word, try to use mental substitutes that are easier to understand.

The Trap of Familiarity

Don't just choose a word because you recognize it. On difficult questions, you may not recognize a number of words in the answer choices. The test writers don't put "make-believe" words on the test; so don't think that just because you only recognize all the words in one answer choice means that answer choice must be correct. If you only recognize words in one answer choice, then focus on that one. Is it correct? Try your best to determine if it is correct. If it is, that is great, but if it doesn't, eliminate it. Each word and answer choice you eliminate increases your chances of getting the question correct, even if you then have to guess among the unfamiliar choices.

Eliminate Answers

Eliminate choices as soon as you realize they are wrong. But be careful! Make sure you consider all of the possible answer choices. Just because one appears right, doesn't mean that the next one won't be even better! The test writers will usually put more than one good answer choice for every question, so read all of them. Don't worry if you are stuck between two that seem right. By getting down to just two remaining possible choices, your odds are now 50/50. Rather than wasting too much time, play the odds. You are guessing, but guessing wisely, because you've been able to knock out some of the answer choices that you know are wrong. If you are eliminating choices and realize that the last answer choice you are left with is also obviously wrong, don't panic. Start over and consider each choice again. There may easily be something that you missed the first time and will realize on the second pass.

Tough Questions

If you are stumped on a problem or it appears too hard or too difficult, don't waste time. Move on! Remember though, if you can quickly check for obviously incorrect answer choices, your chances of guessing correctly are greatly improved. Before you completely give up, at least try to knock out a couple of possible answers. Eliminate what you can and then guess at the remaining answer choices before moving on.

Brainstorm

If you get stuck on a difficult question, spend a few seconds quickly brainstorming. Run through the complete list of possible answer choices. Look at each choice and ask yourself, "Could this answer the question satisfactorily?" Go through each answer choice and consider it independently of the other. By systematically going through all possibilities, you may find something that you would otherwise overlook. Remember that when you get stuck, it's important to try to keep moving.

Read Carefully

Understand the problem. Read the question and answer choices carefully. Don't miss the question because you misread the terms. You have plenty of time to read each question thoroughly and make sure you understand what is being asked. Yet a happy medium must be attained, so don't waste too much time. You must read carefully, but efficiently.

Face Value

When in doubt, use common sense. Always accept the situation in the problem at face value. Don't read too much into it. These problems will not require you to make huge leaps of logic. The test writers aren't trying to throw you off with a cheap trick. If you have to go beyond creativity and make a leap of logic in order to have an answer choice answer the question, then you should look at the other answer choices. Don't overcomplicate the problem by creating theoretical relationships or explanations that will warp time or space.

These are normal problems rooted in reality. It's just that the applicable relationship or explanation may not be readily apparent and you have to figure things out. Use your common sense to interpret anything that isn't clear.

Prefixes

If you're having trouble with a word in the question or answer choices, try dissecting it. Take advantage of every clue that the word might include. Prefixes and suffixes can be a huge help. Usually they allow you to determine a basic meaning. Pre- means before, post- means after, pro - is positive, de- is negative. From these prefixes and suffixes, you can get an idea of the general meaning of the word and try to put it into context. Beware though of any traps. Just because con is the opposite of pro, doesn't necessarily mean congress is the opposite of progress!

Hedge Phrases

Watch out for critical "hedge" phrases, such as likely, may, can, will often, sometimes, often, almost, mostly, usually, generally, rarely, sometimes. Question writers insert these hedge phrases to cover every possibility. Often an answer choice will be wrong simply because it leaves no room for exception. Avoid answer choices that have definitive words like "exactly," and "always".

Switchback Words

Stay alert for "switchbacks". These are the words and phrases frequently used to alert you to shifts in thought. The most common switchback word is "but". Others include although, however, nevertheless, on the other hand, even though, while, in spite of, despite, regardless of.

New Information

Correct answer choices will rarely have completely new information included. Answer choices typically are straightforward reflections of the material asked about and will directly relate to the question. If a new piece of information is included in an answer choice that doesn't even seem to relate to the topic being asked about, then that answer choice is likely incorrect. All of the information needed to answer the question is usually provided for you, and so you should not have to make guesses that are unsupported or choose answer choices that require unknown information that cannot be reasoned on its own.

Time Management

On technical questions, don't get lost on the technical terms. Don't spend too much time on any one question. If you don't know what a term means, then since you don't have a dictionary, odds are you aren't going to get much further. You should immediately recognize terms as whether or not you know them. If you don't, work with the other clues that you have, the other answer choices and terms provided, but don't waste too much time trying to figure out a difficult term.

Contextual Clues

Look for contextual clues. An answer can be right but not correct. The contextual clues will help you find the answer that is most right and is correct. Understand the context in which a phrase or statement is made. This will help you make important distinctions.

Don't Panic

Panicking will not answer any questions for you. Therefore, it isn't helpful. When you first see the question, if your mind goes blank, take a deep breath. Force yourself to mechanically go through the steps of solving the problem and using the strategies you've learned.

Pace Yourself

Don't get clock fever. It's easy to be overwhelmed when you're looking at a page full of questions, your mind is full of random thoughts and feeling confused, and the clock is ticking down faster than you would like. Calm down and maintain the pace that you have set for yourself. As long as you are on track by monitoring your pace, you are guaranteed to have enough time for yourself. When you get to the last few minutes of the test, it may seem like you won't have enough time left, but if you only have as many questions as you should have left at that point, then you're right on track!

Answer Selection

The best way to pick an answer choice is to eliminate all of those that are wrong, until only one is left and confirm that is the correct answer. Sometimes though, an answer choice may immediately look right. Be careful! Take a second to make sure that the other choices are not equally obvious. Don't make a hasty mistake. There are only two times that you should stop before checking other answers. First is when you are positive that the answer choice you have selected is correct. Second is when time is almost out and you have to make a quick guess!

Check Your Work

Since you will probably not know every term listed and the answer to every question, it is important that you get credit for the ones that you do know. Don't miss any questions through careless mistakes. If at all possible, try to take a second to look back over your answer selection and make sure you've selected the correct answer choice and haven't made a costly careless mistake (such as marking an answer choice that you didn't mean to mark). This quick double check should more than pay for itself in caught mistakes for the time it costs.

Beware of Directly Quoted Answers

Sometimes an answer choice will repeat word for word a portion of the question or reference section. However, beware of such exact duplication – it may be a trap! More than likely, the correct choice will paraphrase or summarize a point, rather than being exactly the same wording.

Slang

Scientific sounding answers are better than slang ones. An answer choice that begins "To compare the outcomes…" is much more likely to be correct than one that begins "Because some people insisted…"

Extreme Statements

Avoid wild answers that throw out highly controversial ideas that are proclaimed as established fact. An answer choice that states the "process should be used in certain situations, if…" is much more likely to be correct than one that states the "process should be discontinued completely." The first is a calm rational statement and doesn't even make a definitive, uncompromising stance, using a hedge word "if" to provide wiggle room, whereas the second choice is a radical idea and far more extreme.

Answer Choice Families

When you have two or more answer choices that are direct opposites or parallels, one of them is usually the correct answer. For instance, if one answer choice states "x increases" and another answer choice states "x decreases" or "y increases," then those two or three answer choices are very similar in construction and fall into the same family of answer choices. A family of answer choices is when two or three answer choices are very similar in construction, and yet often have a directly opposite meaning. Usually the correct answer choice will be in that family of answer choices. The "odd man out" or answer choice that doesn't seem to fit the parallel construction of the other answer choices is more likely to be incorrect.

Special Report: Retaking the Test: What Are Your Chances at Improving Your Score?

After going through the experience of taking a major test, many test takers feel that once is enough. The test usually comes during a period of transition in the test taker's life, and taking the test is only one of a series of important events. With so many distractions and conflicting recommendations, it may be difficult for a test taker to rationally determine whether or not he should retake the test after viewing his scores.

The importance of the test usually only adds to the burden of the retake decision. However, don't be swayed by emotion. There a few simple questions that you can ask yourself to guide you as you try to determine whether a retake would improve your score:

1. What went wrong? Why wasn't your score what you expected?

Can you point to a single factor or problem that you feel caused the low score? Were you sick on test day? Was there an emotional upheaval in your life that caused a distraction? Were you late for the test or not able to use the full time allotment? If you can point to any of these specific, individual problems, then a retake should definitely be considered.

2. Is there enough time to improve?

Many problems that may show up in your score report may take a lot of time for improvement. A deficiency in a particular math skill may require weeks or months of tutoring and studying to improve. If you have enough time to improve an identified weakness, then a retake should definitely be considered.

3. How will additional scores be used? Will a score average, highest score, or most recent score be used?

Different test scores may be handled completely differently. If you've taken the test multiple times, sometimes your highest score is used, sometimes your average score is computed and used, and sometimes your most recent score is used. Make sure you understand what method will be used to evaluate your scores, and use that to help you determine whether a retake should be considered.

4. Are my practice test scores significantly higher than my actual test score?

If you have taken a lot of practice tests and are consistently scoring at a much higher level than your actual test score, then you should consider a retake. However, if you've taken five practice tests and only one of your scores was higher than your actual test score, or if your practice test scores were only slightly higher than your actual test score, then it is unlikely that you will significantly increase your score.

5. Do I need perfect scores or will I be able to live with this score? Will this score still allow me to follow my dreams?

What kind of score is acceptable to you? Is your current score "good enough?" Do you have to have a certain score in order to pursue the future of your dreams? If you won't be happy with your current score, and there's no way that you could live with it, then you should consider a retake. However, don't get your hopes up. If you are looking for significant improvement, that may or may not be possible. But if you won't be happy otherwise, it is at least worth the effort.

Remember that there are other considerations. To achieve your dream, it is likely that your grades may also be taken into account. A great test score is usually not the only thing necessary to succeed. Make sure that you aren't overemphasizing the importance of a high test score.

Furthermore, a retake does not always result in a higher score. Some test takers will score lower on a retake, rather than higher. One study shows that one-fourth of test takers will achieve a significant improvement in test score, while one-sixth of test takers will actually show a decrease. While this shows that most test takers will improve, the majority will only improve their scores a little and a retake may not be worth the test taker's effort.

Finally, if a test is taken only once and is considered in the added context of good grades on the part of a test taker, the person reviewing the grades and scores may be tempted to assume that the test taker just had a bad day while taking the test, and may discount the low test score in favor of the high grades. But if the test is retaken and the scores are approximately the same, then the validity of the low scores are only confirmed. Therefore, a retake could actually hurt a test taker by definitely bracketing a test taker's score ability to a limited range.

Special Report: What is Test Anxiety and How to Overcome It?

The very nature of tests caters to some level of anxiety, nervousness or tension, just as we feel for any important event that occurs in our lives. A little bit of anxiety or nervousness can be a good thing. It helps us with motivation, and makes achievement just that much sweeter. However, too much anxiety can be a problem; especially if it hinders our ability to function and perform.

"Test anxiety," is the term that refers to the emotional reactions that some test-takers experience when faced with a test or exam. Having a fear of testing and exams is based upon a rational fear, since the test-taker's performance can shape the course of an academic career. Nevertheless, experiencing excessive fear of examinations will only interfere with the test-takers ability to perform, and his/her chances to be successful.

There are a large variety of causes that can contribute to the development and sensation of test anxiety. These include, but are not limited to lack of performance and worrying about issues surrounding the test.

Lack of Preparation

Lack of preparation can be identified by the following behaviors or situations:

Not scheduling enough time to study, and therefore cramming the night before the test or exam

Managing time poorly, to create the sensation that there is not enough time to do everything

Failing to organize the text information in advance, so that the study material consists of the entire text and not simply the pertinent information

Poor overall studying habits

Worrying, on the other hand, can be related to both the test taker, or many other factors around him/her that will be affected by the results of the test. These include worrying about:

Previous performances on similar exams, or exams in general

How friends and other students are achieving

The negative consequences that will result from a poor grade or failure

There are three primary elements to test anxiety. Physical components, which involve the same typical bodily reactions as those to acute anxiety (to be discussed below). Emotional factors have to do with fear or panic. Mental or cognitive issues concerning attention spans and memory abilities.

Physical Signals

There are many different symptoms of test anxiety, and these are not limited to mental and emotional strain. Frequently there are a range of physical signals that will let a test taker know that he/she is suffering from test anxiety. These bodily changes can include the following:

Perspiring

Sweaty palms

Wet, trembling hands

Nausea

Dry mouth

A knot in the stomach

Headache

Faintness

Muscle tension

Aching shoulders, back and neck

Rapid heart beat

Feeling too hot/cold

To recognize the sensation of test anxiety, a test-taker should monitor him/herself for the following sensations:

The physical distress symptoms as listed above

Emotional sensitivity, expressing emotional feelings such as the need to cry or laugh too much, or a sensation of anger or helplessness

A decreased ability to think, causing the test-taker to blank out or have racing thoughts that are hard to organize or control.

Though most students will feel some level of anxiety when faced with a test or exam, the majority can cope with that anxiety and maintain it at a manageable level. However, those who cannot are faced with a very real and very serious condition, which can and should be controlled for the immeasurable benefit of this sufferer.

Naturally, these sensations lead to negative results for the testing experience. The most common effects of test anxiety have to do with nervousness and mental blocking.

Nervousness

Nervousness can appear in several different levels:

The test-taker's difficulty, or even inability to read and understand the questions on the test

The difficulty or inability to organize thoughts to a coherent form

The difficulty or inability to recall key words and concepts relating to the testing questions (especially essays)

The receipt of poor grades on a test, though the test material was well known by the test taker

Conversely, a person may also experience mental blocking, which involves:

Blanking out on test questions
Only remembering the correct answers to the questions when the test has already finished.

Fortunately for test anxiety sufferers, beating these feelings, to a large degree, has to do with proper preparation. When a test taker has a feeling of preparedness, then anxiety will be dramatically lessened.

The first step to resolving anxiety issues is to distinguish which of the two types of anxiety are being suffered. If the anxiety is a direct result of a lack of preparation, this should be considered a normal reaction, and the anxiety level (as opposed to the test results) shouldn't be anything to worry about. However, if, when adequately prepared, the test-taker still panics, blanks out, or seems to overreact, this is not a fully rational reaction. While this can be considered normal too, there are many ways to combat and overcome these effects.

Remember that anxiety cannot be entirely eliminated, however, there are ways to minimize it, to make the anxiety easier to manage. Preparation is one of the best ways to minimize test anxiety. Therefore the following techniques are wise in order to best fight off any anxiety that may want to build.

To begin with, try to avoid cramming before a test, whenever it is possible. By trying to memorize an entire term's worth of information in one day, you'll be shocking your system, and not giving yourself a very good chance to absorb the information. This is an easy path to anxiety, so for those who suffer from test anxiety, cramming should not even be considered an option.

Instead of cramming, work throughout the semester to combine all of the material which is presented throughout the semester, and work on it gradually as the course goes by, making sure to master the main concepts first, leaving minor details for a week or so before the test.

To study for the upcoming exam, be sure to pose questions that may be on the examination, to gauge the ability to answer them by integrating the ideas from your texts, notes and lectures, as well as any supplementary readings.

If it is truly impossible to cover all of the information that was covered in that particular term, concentrate on the most important portions, that can be covered very well. Learn these concepts as best as possible, so that when the test comes, a goal can be made to use these concepts as presentations of your knowledge.

In addition to study habits, changes in attitude are critical to beating a struggle with test anxiety. In fact, an improvement of the perspective over the entire test-taking experience can actually help a test taker to enjoy studying and therefore improve the overall experience. Be certain not to overemphasize the significance of the grade - know that the result of the test is neither a reflection of self worth, nor is it a measure of intelligence; one grade will not predict a person's future success.

To improve an overall testing outlook, the following steps should be tried:

Keeping in mind that the most reasonable expectation for taking a test is to expect to try to demonstrate as much of what you know as you possibly can.
Reminding ourselves that a test is only one test; this is not the only one, and there will be others.

The thought of thinking of oneself in an irrational, all-or-nothing term should be avoided at all costs.

A reward should be designated for after the test, so there's something to look forward to. Whether it be going to a movie, going out to eat, or simply visiting friends, schedule it in advance, and do it no matter what result is expected on the exam.

Test-takers should also keep in mind that the basics are some of the most important things, even beyond anti-anxiety techniques and studying. Never neglect the basic social, emotional and biological needs, in order to try to absorb information. In order to best achieve, these three factors must be held as just as important as the studying itself.

Study Steps

Remember the following important steps for studying:

Maintain healthy nutrition and exercise habits. Continue both your recreational activities and social pass times. These both contribute to your physical and emotional well being.

Be certain to get a good amount of sleep, especially the night before the test, because when you're overtired you are not able to perform to the best of your best ability.

Keep the studying pace to a moderate level by taking breaks when they are needed, and varying the work whenever possible, to keep the mind fresh instead of getting bored.

When enough studying has been done that all the material that can be learned has been learned, and the test taker is prepared for the test, stop studying and do something relaxing such as listening to music, watching a movie, or taking a warm bubble bath.

There are also many other techniques to minimize the uneasiness or apprehension that is experienced along with test anxiety before, during, or even after the examination. In fact, there are a great deal of things that can be done to stop anxiety from interfering with lifestyle and performance. Again, remember that anxiety will not be eliminated entirely, and it shouldn't be. Otherwise that "up" feeling for exams would not exist, and most of us depend on that sensation to perform better than usual. However, this anxiety has to be at a level that is manageable.

Of course, as we have just discussed, being prepared for the exam is half the battle right away. Attending all classes, finding out what knowledge will be expected on the exam, and knowing the exam schedules are easy steps to lowering anxiety. Keeping up with work will remove the need to cram, and efficient study habits will eliminate wasted time. Studying should be done in an ideal location for concentration, so that it is simple to become interested in the material and give it complete attention. A method such as SQ3R (Survey, Question, Read, Recite, Review) is a wonderful key to follow to make sure that the study habits are as effective as possible, especially in the case of learning from a textbook. Flashcards are great techniques for memorization. Learning to take good notes will mean that notes will be full of useful information, so that less sifting will need to be done to seek out what is pertinent for studying. Reviewing notes after class and then again on occasion will keep the information fresh in the mind. From notes that have been taken summary sheets and outlines can be made for simpler reviewing.

A study group can also be a very motivational and helpful place to study, as there will be a sharing of ideas, all of the minds can work together, to make sure that everyone understands, and the studying will be made more interesting because it will be a social occasion.

Basically, though, as long as the test-taker remains organized and self confident, with efficient study habits, less time will need to be spent studying, and higher grades will be achieved.

To become self confident, there are many useful steps. The first of these is "self talk." It has been shown through extensive research, that self-talk for students who suffer from test anxiety, should be well monitored, in order to make sure that it contributes to self confidence as opposed to sinking the student. Frequently the self talk of test-anxious students is negative or self-defeating, thinking that everyone else is smarter and faster, that they always mess up, and that if they don't do well, they'll fail the entire course. It is important to decreasing anxiety that awareness is made of self talk. Try writing any negative self thoughts and then disputing them with a positive statement instead. Begin self-encouragement as though it was a friend speaking. Repeat positive statements to help reprogram the mind to believing in successes instead of failures.

Helpful Techniques

Other extremely helpful techniques include:

Self-visualization of doing well and reaching goals
While aiming for an "A" level of understanding, don't try to "overprotect" by setting your expectations lower. This will only convince the mind to stop studying in order to meet the lower expectations.
Don't make comparisons with the results or habits of other students. These are individual factors, and different things work for different people, causing different results.
Strive to become an expert in learning what works well, and what can be done in order to improve. Consider collecting this data in a journal.
Create rewards for after studying instead of doing things before studying that will only turn into avoidance behaviors.
Make a practice of relaxing - by using methods such as progressive relaxation, self-hypnosis, guided imagery, etc - in order to make relaxation an automatic sensation.
Work on creating a state of relaxed concentration so that concentrating will take on the focus of the mind, so that none will be wasted on worrying.
Take good care of the physical self by eating well and getting enough sleep.
Plan in time for exercise and stick to this plan.

Beyond these techniques, there are other methods to be used before, during and after the test that will help the test-taker perform well in addition to overcoming anxiety.

Before the exam comes the academic preparation. This involves establishing a study schedule and beginning at least one week before the actual date of the test. By doing this, the anxiety of not having enough time to study for the test will be automatically eliminated. Moreover, this will make the studying a much more effective experience, ensuring that the learning will be an easier process. This relieves much undue pressure on the test-taker.

Summary sheets, note cards, and flash cards with the main concepts and examples of these main concepts should be prepared in advance of the actual studying time. A topic should never be eliminated from this process. By omitting a topic because it isn't expected to be on the test is only setting up the test-taker for anxiety should it actually appear on the exam. Utilize the course syllabus for laying out the topics that should be studied. Carefully go over the notes that were made in class, paying special attention to any of the issues that the professor took special care to emphasize while lecturing in class. In the textbooks, use the chapter review, or if possible, the chapter tests, to begin your review.

It may even be possible to ask the instructor what information will be covered on the exam, or what the format of the exam will be (for example, multiple choice, essay, free form, true-false). Additionally, see if it is possible to find out how many questions will be on the test. If a review sheet or sample test has been offered by the professor, make good use of it, above anything else, for the preparation for the test. Another great resource for getting to know the examination is reviewing tests from previous semesters. Use these tests to review, and aim to achieve a 100% score on each of the possible topics. With a few exceptions, the goal that you set for yourself is the highest one that you will reach.

Take all of the questions that were assigned as homework, and rework them to any other possible course material. The more problems reworked, the more skill and confidence will form as a result. When forming the solution to a problem, write out each of the steps. Don't simply do head work. By doing as many steps on paper as possible, much clarification and therefore confidence will be formed. Do this with as many homework problems as possible, before checking the answers. By checking the answer after each problem, a reinforcement will exist, that will not be on the exam. Study situations should be as exam-like as possible, to prime the test-taker's system for the experience. By waiting to check the answers at the end, a psychological advantage will be formed, to decrease the stress factor.

Another fantastic reason for not cramming is the avoidance of confusion in concepts, especially when it comes to mathematics. 8-10 hours of study will become one hundred percent more effective if it is spread out over a week or at least several days, instead of doing it all in one sitting. Recognize that the human brain requires time in order to assimilate new material, so frequent breaks and a span of study time over several days will be much more beneficial.

Additionally, don't study right up until the point of the exam. Studying should stop a minimum of one hour before the exam begins. This allows the brain to rest and put things in their proper order. This will also provide the time to become as relaxed as possible when going into the examination room. The test-taker will also have time to eat well and eat sensibly. Know that the brain needs food as much as the rest of the body. With enough food and enough sleep, as well as a relaxed attitude, the body and the mind are primed for success.

Avoid any anxious classmates who are talking about the exam. These students only spread anxiety, and are not worth sharing the anxious sentimentalities.

Before the test also involves creating a positive attitude, so mental preparation should also be a point of concentration. There are many keys to creating a positive attitude. Should fears become rushing in, make a visualization of taking the exam, doing well, and seeing an A written on the paper. Write out a list of affirmations that will bring a feeling of confidence, such as "I am doing well in my English class," "I studied well and know my material," "I enjoy this class." Even if the affirmations aren't believed at first, it sends a positive message to the subconscious which will result in an alteration of the overall belief system, which is the system that creates reality.

If a sensation of panic begins, work with the fear and imagine the very worst! Work through the entire scenario of not passing the test, failing the entire course, and dropping out of school, followed by not getting a job, and pushing a shopping cart through the dark alley where you'll live. This will place things into perspective! Then, practice deep breathing and create a visualization of the opposite situation - achieving an "A" on the exam, passing the entire course, receiving the degree at a graduation ceremony.

On the day of the test, there are many things to be done to ensure the best results, as well as the most calm outlook. The following stages are suggested in order to maximize test-taking potential:

Begin the examination day with a moderate breakfast, and avoid any coffee or beverages with caffeine if the test taker is prone to jitters. Even people who are used to managing caffeine can feel jittery or light-headed when it is taken on a test day. Attempt to do something that is relaxing before the examination begins. As last minute cramming clouds the mastering of overall concepts, it is better to use this time to create a calming outlook.
Be certain to arrive at the test location well in advance, in order to provide time to select a location that is away from doors, windows and other distractions, as well as giving enough time to relax before the test begins.

Keep away from anxiety generating classmates who will upset the sensation of stability and relaxation that is being attempted before the exam.

Should the waiting period before the exam begins cause anxiety, create a self-distraction by reading a light magazine or something else that is relaxing and simple.

During the exam itself, read the entire exam from beginning to end, and find out how much time should be allotted to each individual problem. Once writing the exam, should more time be taken for a problem, it should be abandoned, in order to begin another problem. If there is time at the end, the unfinished problem can always be returned to and completed.

Read the instructions very carefully - twice - so that unpleasant surprises won't follow during or after the exam has ended.

When writing the exam, pretend that the situation is actually simply the completion of homework within a library, or at home. This will assist in forming a relaxed atmosphere, and will allow the brain extra focus for the complex thinking function.

Begin the exam with all of the questions with which the most confidence is felt. This will build the confidence level regarding the entire exam and will begin a quality momentum. This will also create encouragement for trying the problems where uncertainty resides.

Going with the "gut instinct" is always the way to go when solving a problem. Second guessing should be avoided at all costs. Have confidence in the ability to do well.

For essay questions, create an outline in advance that will keep the mind organized and make certain that all of the points are remembered. For multiple choice, read every answer, even if the correct one has been spotted - a better one may exist.

Continue at a pace that is reasonable and not rushed, in order to be able to work carefully. Provide enough time to go over the answers at the end, to check for small errors that can be corrected.

Should a feeling of panic begin, breathe deeply, and think of the feeling of the body releasing sand through its pores. Visualize a calm, peaceful place, and include all of the sights, sounds and sensations of this image. Continue the deep breathing, and take a few minutes to continue this with closed eyes. When all is well again, return to the test.

If a "blanking" occurs for a certain question, skip it and move on to the next question. There will be time to return to the other question later. Get everything done that can be done, first, to guarantee all the grades that can be compiled, and to build all of the confidence possible. Then return to the weaker questions to build the marks from there.

Remember, one's own reality can be created, so as long as the belief is there, success will follow. And remember: anxiety can happen later, right now, there's an exam to be written!

After the examination is complete, whether there is a feeling for a good grade or a bad grade, don't dwell on the exam, and be certain to follow through on the reward that was promised...and enjoy it! Don't dwell on any mistakes that have been made, as there is nothing that can be done at this point anyway.

Additionally, don't begin to study for the next test right away. Do something relaxing for a while, and let the mind relax and prepare itself to begin absorbing information again.

From the results of the exam - both the grade and the entire experience, be certain to learn from what has gone on. Perfect studying habits and work some more on

- 112 -

confidence in order to make the next examination experience even better than the last one.

Learn to avoid places where openings occurred for laziness, procrastination and day dreaming.

Use the time between this exam and the next one to better learn to relax, even learning to relax on cue, so that any anxiety can be controlled during the next exam. Learn how to relax the body. Slouch in your chair if that helps. Tighten and then relax all of the different muscle groups, one group at a time, beginning with the feet and then working all the way up to the neck and face. This will ultimately relax the muscles more than they were to begin with. Learn how to breathe deeply and comfortably, and focus on this breathing going in and out as a relaxing thought. With every exhale, repeat the word "relax."

As common as test anxiety is, it is very possible to overcome it. Make yourself one of the test-takers who overcome this frustrating hindrance.

Special Report: Additional Bonus Material

Due to our efforts to try to keep this book to a manageable length, we've created a link that will give you access to all of your additional bonus material.

Please visit http://www.mometrix.com/bonus948/toeflibt to access the information.